Can the *Tao Te Ching* change your life?
No.
Only you can change your way.

Can the *Tao Te Ching* change your attitude?
Maybe
If you make its suggestions part of your life

Read a few of these pages
Try on a few of these ideas
You don't have to change your core beliefs.

But when you change your attitude
you'll change your life.

And you can also read
a few of these pages
if you want to learn

- How to pronounce *Tao* – and why we say it that way.
- How Peking became Beijing.
- The joy of anonymity.
- How procrastination can be good for you.

In brief, this is a self-help book that encourages you to practice non-action.

It's your day, make it your Tao

A travel companion for your personal path through life

James Patrick Maney

It's Your Day, Make It Your Tao – A travel companion for your personal path through life © 2014-2021 by James Patrick Maney
Cover and chapter title photography © James Patrick Maney
Portions of this book have appeared on https://tao-not-dow.org/ and https://yourdayyourtao.org/ .

All rights reserved. No part of this book may be reproduced or transmitted in any form by any means, electronic or mechanical, including photocopying, recording or by any information storage and retrieval system, without permission in writing from the author. This book may not be circulated without a cover or in any cover other than the existing cover.

Published by an cosán press
info@yourdayyourtao.org

ISBN 978-1-7365679-3-7 (sc)
ISBN 978-1-7365679-2-0 (hc)
ISBN 978-1-7365679-1-3 (e)

Contents

Before the beginning..xiii

Getting Started..1
- What's the *Tao Te Ching*? – Condensing 2500 years of history to a few pages.
- *Tao* or *Dao?* What's the difference?

The Sage..11
- Who's a Sage?
- Is there a "best" translation of the *Tao*?
- Suggestions for reading this section
- Becoming a Sage - verses and exercises

Te, **or Virtue**...77
- *Te*, defining virtue in the *Tao Te Ching*
- How to find and define your own version of virtue
- Practicing Te, or virtue – verses and exercises

Wu-Wei, **or non-action**...115
- *Wu-Wei*, an overview
- Practicing Wu-Wei, or non-action – verses and exercises

Acknowledgements..150

Verses indexed by topic...152

Topics indexed by verse..153

Social media notes..154

About the Author..155

Before this book's beginning. . .

The longer I live, the more I appreciate the paths my life has taken. Sure, there have been bumps, breakdowns and plans gone awry. And those times when you feel the bottom fall out of your stomach and have no idea what to do with this sudden void in your life. But there have also been surprise opportunities leading to wonderful people and places I'd never have imagined or planned years ago. Overall, I've been fortunate, even though there were times when I didn't have this perspective on life that time has brought me. In the business world, people have paid me to learn, travel and share my experiences with them. Learning about other people's lives and businesses has helped me to help them. Years of travel, study, consulting and teaching in one form or another have [hopefully] allowed me to be somewhat objective in dealing with things while recognizing my own limitations. Do I have biases? Of course. We all do. Mine will become obvious as we travel this book's *Tao* – its way – together.

Learning from the locals – whether in my days working on a factory floor, in the middle of the Australian outback, the African desert, the Andes, or in offices and conference rooms across North America – has given me perspectives and habits that I've kept to this day. I travel light. Whether it's a laptop and overnight bag or just a backpack, if it doesn't fit in the overhead, I don't need it. [Both my army and my backpacking days taught me to prioritize how much I can carry for long distances on my back.]

Since I know that we can't take anything with us when we leave this planet, I choose to spend my resources on experiences instead of stuff and rent on places to store said stuff.

While my journey – or series of learning experiences – began in childhood, this book began when a friend gave me a clothbound hardcover copy of the *Tao Te Ching* with beautiful photography accompanying each verse. I found myself drooling over the photos and dreaming of ways to get to China. But with a few exceptions, the book's verses just didn't grab me and the accompanying commentary was a bit too academic for my tastes and knowledge at that time. I've never made it to China [except for three hours in an airport lounge on a layover between Sydney and Amsterdam], but the gift planted a seed that sprouted years later with books that jumped off shelves at me and commentaries sitting in used book bins waiting for me to find them. And of course there's life's synchronicity where one new thing leads to another and all of a sudden you're immersed in things you never knew existed. These experiences were followed by questions from people who thought I knew more than they did. Their questions that led me to more homework. The results became this book and its accompanying website [https://yourdayyourtao.org/]. I hope you find them useful companions on your own journey.

But remember, my *Tao* may not be your *Tao*. We all come from different environments and have different personalities that have led us into different lifestyles.

The advantage of the *Tao Te Ching* is that [1] it's in verse, with lots of imagery we can interpret as we wish and [2] it's translated into today's alphabets from an ideographic language that's been obsolete for a few thousand years. Each translation you find is an opinion, not a fact.

So, take what you want from the *Tao* and make it your own. But more importantly, once you make it your own, make it your own habit. The *Tao* is a roadside guide, not a gospel.

Getting Started

Let's face it, for most of us, today's *Tao Te Ching* resources are somewhat intimidating.

There are countless translations of the *Tao Te Ching* – and even more interpretations. Their sheer volume can easily dissuade all but the most dedicated from exploring this wonderful resource. One solution? Browse a nearby store's bookshelves until you find a copy that feels right, one that resonates with you. Keep it by your side as you read what's here – and develop your own interpretations. After all, my path [my *Tao*] may not be yours.

Don't be surprised if you find yourself looking for – and at – different versions of the book as you travel along your path in life. You don't see things today as you did ten years ago. Hopefully, your viewpoints will mature to a different stage as you learn from life over the next ten years.

You might want to look at any version of the *Tao Te Ching* as a guidebook, not a gospel. The guidebook to a country that you read at home may help you make a travel decision, but won't be much help when you're standing on a street corner in a foreign place looking for a particular address. Whether your teacher is a book, a recording, or a real live person, you'll find that your needs – and your wants from your teachers – will evolve as you learn.

What's my own travel plan?

To create a plain English response to the *Tao Te Ching* for today's times.

So . . . here we'll still see the *Tao Te Ching*'s thoughts, meanings and reflections, but in a format that may be easier for this century's Western eyes. We'll touch on many topics. Nearly every sentence or paragraph can lead to another conversation, another viewpoint, another path. Consider these chapters to be thought-starters, not answers. If, while you're reading, your mind wanders down another path, adapting my words to your experiences, by all means follow its footsteps. My words will still be on the page, your mind's images may be fleeting. [So write them down!]

The *Tao Te Ching* wasn't written in the form most of us see today. Many verses contain multiple unrelated topics while adjoining chapters complement or complete each other. In addition, the *Tao Te Ching* has a series of recurring themes, reinforcing messages in different contexts in different verses throughout the document. I'm approaching the *Tao* in a way that's somewhat different from others, exploring the *Tao*'s themes as they develop and evolve through the book. While I'll reference the source chapters I'm using at the top of their pages, they'll be organized by theme, rather than by number.

Taoism isn't about changing your beliefs, it's about adjusting your attitude.

Taoism isn't a religion like Judaism, Christianity, Islam or other beliefs. It was a worldview already in existence by the time Buddhism reached China, where they found many attitudes in common.

Taoism doesn't deal with the unknowable – creation and the creator. Instead, it talks of the best ways of dealing with the creation we're part of. It leaves discussions of angels and pinheads to those with extra time on their hands, focusing instead on how to live in the everyday world. For better or worse, today's society has a lot in common with Chinese society of 2500 years ago.

The written Chinese language of the *Tao* didn't use gender. And it was replaced by another form of writing several hundred years later. Today we use gender references as a means of convenience, as do most translators. Please recognize that, if you pick up an older translation, the consistent use of "he" and other male references are more a reflection of the translator's times and culture than of the *Tao's* original content. Of course, we also have to recognize the roles of males and females in the Chinese culture of its origin. Naturally the better translators and interpreters will admit the difficulties and deficiencies inherent in working from a dead language created by the literate class of an ancient culture.

Where do we start?

The world's major belief systems identify an individual creator, giving this entity specific personality traits and detailing the creation of the world we know in terms of the mythos, science and societies of their day. The *Tao* doesn't.

The *Tao Te Ching* reflects the society of its creation: China in the Second Millennium BCE. But it refuses to identify a creator, because identification limits the god-being we name. To borrow from J.B.S. Haldane's *Possible Worlds*, "the universe is not only queerer than we suppose, but queerer than we can suppose." As we learn in *Tao's* first verse, whatever we name becomes limited by our definition.

The *Tao Te Ching* is not a creation story, but rather a guidebook on how to deal with universal issues that arise in society – dealing with life and the universe we inhabit.

It recognizes that the universe exists and then proceeds to suggest how we should deal with it – and with each other – since we're all part of the same universe.

My *Tao* isn't the original *Tao* – or your *Tao*, either

The *Tao Te Ching* is a 2500-year-old collection of aphorisms attributed to Lao Tzu, a composite person positioned as a flower child against an imperial Confucian monarchy that emphasized rules and regulations to maintain law and order. Neither archetype is totally accurate, but they're close enough for our current purposes. Please feel free to do additional homework on the cultural backgrounds of Confucianism and Taoism and how they fit into the society of their time.

The title – *Tao Te Ching* – translates into many different things, all dependent on the translator's skill and intent, as well as our own perceptions. It can be loosely translated into The Book [*Ching*] of the Way [*Tao*] of Virtue [*Te*]. Or, the Book of The Way and its Virtue.

The Chinese glyph for *Tao* can be read as either a noun or a verb, depending on context, variously reading as a way or a guide. As a group, we can all walk the same path and experience different things. As individuals, we can walk the same path many times, learning different things from it each time.

The *Tao* is rich in context-driven irony. In today's culture it even shares a homonym with the Dow, a capitalist icon it can easily be used to mock. Whether we read it in the context of today or two millennia ago, the *Tao* isn't clean, pretty and full of life-affirming aphorisms. It's a sarcastic, ironic, Machiavellian collection of metaphors, many of which run several layers deep, creating different meanings for different readers. Many times these comments are made through paradox. Taking its metaphors for gospel and its comments without context may not take you on a path you'd prefer. When we consider the times and context of its origin, much of its meaning was forced to remain between its lines, in the same manner subsequent cultures embedded political commentary in benign-appearing entertainment. [Nursery rhyme *Mary Mary Quite Contrary*, Swift's *Modest Proposal* and the more recent *Alice in Wonderland*, *Animal Farm* and *M*A*S*H* are just a few of the many examples we can use.]

Can we truly explain the *Tao*?

No.

How many times have we said, "You had to be there" when we're talking about an event or physical phenomenon – a sunrise, sunset, joke, meeting, particular taste or sensation? There are countless translations of the *Tao*. The face value of a passage may or may not convey the true meaning of a chapter. Scholars disagree. And the more you know, the more you know that you don't know all there is to know and that you need to know more…

Back to my *Tao* for today's world –

The comments on these pages have evolved through the years, changing to reflect my new understandings, my new impressions of the larger path we all share in this lifetime. While I've tried to stay true to the *Tao's* meaning, these posts reflect my experience with each of its precepts, which may or may not be their original intent. For the most part, these pieces are written in clear, everyday language, not the stilted academic one that translators sometimes adopt, since it's their natural way of communicating among themselves. A few thousand years ago these verses were written in the conversational language of their time, not the formal language of Confucian courts. I hope you find them useful. The photos and backgrounds come from my personal photos, created as I've walked my own path.

In brief, these are not translations, but rather responses inspired by the *Tao* – not the Dow. Undoubtedly there are some good Dowists out there. And if you are, you'll find some excellent tactical and strategic advice in a significant number of the *Tao's* verses. Enjoy your search.

Tao or *Dao*? What's the difference?

There isn't any, except in western spelling and individual preference.

If you've wandered the web, bookshops, or the world, you may have come across many of the things we're talking about here under the name of *Dao De Jing*. In either spelling, the word is pronounced DOW, as in Dow-Jones. Chinese is a tonal language with hundreds of dialects. As with any language, different native speakers pronounce the same words in different ways – and non-native speakers apply their own ears and rules to what they hear.

Getting Started

No matter the language, most learners of a foreign tongue instinctively apply the rules of pronunciation and word formation that they learned in their first language. It may not be correct, but it's intuitive, particularly among those who insist on reading, rather than speaking a new language at the beginning. Here's a simple experiment for you: Pronounce the letter "D". Notice where your tongue falls in your mouth and how your breath flows. Now pronounce the letter "T". Then repeat "duh" and "tuh" several times in succession. See how close their formations are? Now use what you've just learned as part of a word, not as a syllable by itself. Then use that word in a sentence. Confused yet? Remember that now you need to both create and distinguish the rising and falling inflections in the Chinese language, a task that can be somewhat difficult for western ears.

We find another source of the difference in the two spellings in western transliteration history. The Wade-Giles romanization of the Beijing dialect of Mandarin Chinese was developed in the latter 19th century and used for most of the 20th. Wade and Giles were British diplomats stationed in China, using their English ears to match appropriate sounds to the language and alphabet of their homeland. It's the source of *Tao* spelling, with the letter T.

Pinyin is a more recent effort to convert Chinese symbols to the Roman alphabet, developed by Chinese in the latter 20th century. For example, the city of Beijing is the Pinyin version of the Wade-Giles Peking. [Peking received its spelling from French missionaries in the 17th and 18th centuries. Wade and Giles decided to keep it.] *Dao* is the Pinyin spelling of *Tao*. The names *Lao Tzu*, *Laozi* and *Lao-Tze* all refer to the same person, spelled according to the westernized ear of the speaker. This name, usually used to refer to the author of the *Tao Te Ching*, is actually a title or honorific meaning *Old Master*.

You mean that there's really no other difference between the two spellings?

Among devotees of one form of Taoism or another, there are good people who will disagree with me. Think for a moment of referring to a person as a Christian, Muslim or Jew. From the outside looking in, it's usually a suitable general label. But the Catholic, Lutheran, Sunni, Shia, Orthodox or Reform member of a group may differ with you and point out why you may want to readjust your thinking.

A legacy of Wade-Giles is that the "T" spelling of *Tao* is generally more prevalent in popular culture. Taoism, like many other philosophies, has evolved through the centuries. Part of this evolution comes from its movement into different cultures, where local norms, language and views supplant those of the source. Even though they are part of the same tree, does every branch on a tree look like every other one? A natural forest consists of many species of plant life. To the outsider, it's a forest. The botanist – or the tree whose roots are in constant communication with others of its genus and species – may disagree with you.

Taoism's roots lie in the Shamanic traditions of ancient China. Along the way it's branched into the philosophical Taoism we'll be using here and other, more structured, religious expressions of its principles. As you travel your own *Tao*, you may encounter Taoists who resemble Buddhists, or others who practice mysticism, meditation and different techniques that help them connect to the world we all share. Just as we can find our way to a destination on multi-laned paved motorways, barely-discernible footpaths and many other routes in between, consider *Tao* to be a generic name for the paths we travel in life. My *Tao* may not be your *Tao*. But each of our paths is right for our own journey through life.

Anyway,

the "T" spelling of *Tao* is generally more prevalent in popular western culture. Remember I'm not translating the *Tao Te Ching*, but using it as an inspiration for comments on today's life.

So, I'll respect the Daoists, but stay with *Tao*.

Who's a Sage?

Is a Sage simply a wise person?
A holy man?
A saint?
A philosopher?
The power behind the throne?
A recognized leader?
An actual leader?

Or just an ordinary person acting in accordance with the *Tao Te Ching* – someone whose actions are in complete harmony with their environment?

In *Tao*, as in so many other areas of life, everything depends on context. Where verses specifically mention a Sage, they cast this person sometimes as a leader, sometimes as a viewer of life, sometimes as a student, sometimes conflating several roles in the same verse.

The answer to the question of "Who – or what – is a Sage," is, "It depends."

What many translators call a sage is known in China as a Shengren [Zhenren]. Like many concepts Westerners encounter in Oriental societies, the Shengren has no true equivalent in Western culture. So we need to rely on the translator's own view of the Chinese character and its context. As with the words of many languages, Chinese characters have shades of meaning, many of which are conveyed through context and the inflections of speech rather than the fixity of writing. And don't forget synonyms, which may be close, but not exactly the same, as our target word. In my teaching days I sometimes cringed over the results of students pulling words from a thesaurus in an effort to impress me. I'll have to admit, they did impress me – with their ignorance of the actual meaning of the word they used. Just because a word is in a thesaurus list doesn't mean it's an exact match for the meaning you're trying to convey.

Want to cast some more doubt on the meaning of translated Chinese words? Much of the early translation was done by European missionaries, each of whom viewed the text through their own particular lens and agenda, creating sages as leaders, wise men and saints with varying degrees of stature in their societies. Oh, and the documents they worked from used a Chinese alphabet that didn't exist when the *Tao* was composed, but one that was imposed on the language several hundred years later.

While today's translators may not be viewing the text through stained-glass lenses, they still bring their own perspective, preconceived notions and cultural biases to the project. Like us, they're human. Some translations use the term wise, wise person or master instead of sage. This can lend itself to the concept of an influencer, leader or ruler rather than one of the people. It doesn't need to be a political ruler. Sometimes it can be a respected elder, or one recognized for their wisdom. Chinese meaning depends on word order.

So, what are we to do with all of this confusion?

Use *Tao* as you'd use a map showing several ways to reach the same place. Or as your memory of a guide's verbal directions, complete with landmarks that may no longer be on your way. Find a translation that resonates with you. Or a commentary. Or a response in the vein that you'll see here, where I use verses that resonate with me as jumping off points on the trail of life.

Then follow your path. Even if it's not the same as mine, it'll be the one that's right for you.

Some suggestions for reading this section –

First, a few more words on translating Chinese into English. Then you'll see my own responses to each of the *Tao*'s verses that specifically mention a Sage. If you agree with me, wonderful! If you don't, wonderful! In that case I hope you make the time to consider your response to my thoughts or to the *Tao*'s original verse, in whatever form it comes to you. In either case, try to find ways to make your response part of your own life on your own *Tao*.

And if you'd like to follow the concept of Sagehood down a rabbit hole of research, ask your search engine to look up Zhenren or Shengren. The root word Zhen/Sheng is generally westernized as holy, or perfected, or genuine, or some other description that marks the person as exceptionally virtuous or good. The second character refers to the person, in many translations it's "man". But just saying a holy person only puts western blinders on a much broader concept. If you'd rather use Chinese characters, the traditional character is 聖人. The simplified character is 圣人. And while you're at it, take a look at the character for woman and compare it to what you've just discovered. If you're into linguistics, you may even want to do an open-ended search for sage, saint, wise man and similar titles or honorifics. You'll find Chinese characters conveying all these shades of meaning. I'm sure there are countless graduate school theses examining the issue.

Each of the following sections begins with a passage from the verse we'll be working with – along with a number identifying the source verse. While you may want to read them sequentially, I'd suggest that, in the beginning, you just randomly read these notes and the accompanying reflections on *Tao's* verses at your own pace, with or without an accompanying copy of the *Tao Te Ching*. Apply whatever you like to your own life and move on, making your learning part of your life, not your memory.

Or . . .

Get a book – yes, a real book – this will keep you from clicking from screen to screen with a chosen online *Tao*. Make notes in its margins. Writing things down reinforces your thoughts, making them more likely to stay with you. [Reading from paper instead of a screen does the same thing.]

Over the years I've read many versions of the *Tao* and consulted at least as many commentaries. I like some parts of some versions, other parts of others. My excerpts here are synthesized from this research, with an emphasis on contemporary, non-academic English. So find what you like and use my thoughts as thought-starters for yourself.

Note that many of *Tao*'s verses cover several topics, since current versions were collated long after the original document was compiled. Since my approach is thematic rather than numeric, an individual essay may pertain to lines in the middle or the end of a particular verse, or even consecutive verses where a topic is spread between the two. The passage headlining one of my commentaries may not be the one at the beginning of a verse, but rather one from its middle, pertaining to our subject.

Enjoy.
Learn.
Live what you learn.

Becoming a Sage – verses and exercises

Verse 2

The Master acts without doing and teaches without saying.

OK, so the Sage is devoted to "non-action" – does that mean we should sit around and do nothing until our fairy godmother pops in from the ether and taps us with her wand? Of course not! Non-action is one of those translation issues that's become institutionalized through repetition. [See the section on *Wu-wei* for more discussion on the meaning of "non-action".] The Sage – your inner wise person – recognizes that we're part of nature with no need to interfere with natural processes. Then, when the time is right, with minimum effort, the Sage achieves their goal.

For a few moments, don't call yourself a Sage. Become a surfer, instead. You sit on your board, observing, waiting for the right wave. You don't waste your time on the baby waves. And you don't endanger your life on the waves you're not ready for, but you know enough about yourself and local conditions to pick the Goldilocks Wave, the one that's just right for you. Or, if you prefer to stay on dry land, imagine yourself a ju-jitsu practitioner waiting for your opposite to commit to a direction so that when you give them a simple nudge, all their strength and movement accrues to your benefit. Why waste time and energy trying to control what you can't, when you can use your knowledge to control your response to a situation? Note that we're saying response, rather than reaction. Response requires thought and consideration for an outcome. A responder recognizes their environment and deals with it in terms of the outcome they want. Reaction is simply an avoidance mechanism that may provoke a chain of other reactions, many of which may be beyond our control or ability to deal with. It's a distinction you may want to apply when you observe public figures in action.

We also need to recognize that attaching our feelings to anyone or anything can create a whole new set of issues. Ownership, be it of an object or another's feelings, creates responsibilities. These duties can become either steps or stones in our particular path, our *Tao*. The Sage's path is one of freedom. So...should you choose attachments, recognize that they come with a price. Be sure you get what you pay for. Attachments, such as to a particular concept of beauty, place a bias in your viewpoint. To be in *Tao*, the Sage must be beyond bias, accepting everything and everyone on their own terms. The Sage sees beautiful and ugly not as opposites, but as different, as complementary – or two sides of the same coin.

Simply put, if you don't recognize ownership, you don't have to deal with loss. How can you lose what you never had?

Throughout *Tao*, you'll see encouragement to practice modesty. This makes absolute sense, because how can the Sage take credit for something that was already happening of its own accord? Besides, if we listen to our inner Sage, we'll understand that actions unattached to a name are more likely to last longer. They live on their merits, not the fleeting fame or infamy of their creator. There's a quote that's been attributed to quite a few different philosophers and politicians through the years: "There's no limit to the amount of good you can accomplish if you're willing to let someone else take the credit." This principle, a variation on non-action, is woven throughout *Tao*'s verses focusing on the Sage. When no credit is taken, accomplishment endures. It becomes part of everyone's life, not subject to disposal through guilt by association with a previous ruler or time.

We've just covered a lot of ground here. Let's break it down.
- You're probably smart enough to wait for an apple to ripen before you eat it. How can you apply this principle to the work you do every day?
- Do you know the difference between smothering and mothering? Think of the times someone intruded on you when you just needed some quiet time. When have you done the same thing to others? And more importantly, how will you behave on both sides of these situations in days to come?
- How many times have you passed something by, just because you didn't care for the person involved? How many people have done this to you – and how can you improve things?

Verse 3

The leader empties people's minds and hearts by filling their bellies.

Forget today's diet-conscious fixation on stomachs. Instead, look at this commentary metaphorically [remember, the *Tao* is a long verse, not a text book]. How do the wise keep the peace in themselves, their families, their societies? By satisfying basic needs. If you don't, the time may come when people hungry for physical or social satisfaction decide to focus on you as the source of their problems. People on pedestals are easy-to-see targets for the frustrated. [Another reason for the anonymity prized in Verse 2. It's rare that a power behind the throne is identified and vilified.]

The Sage, whether or not they're seen as a leader, fills bellies to keep the peace. Roman rulers of old provided bread and circuses to distract people from civic problems. While entertainment, food, clothing and shelter may fall under the "bellies" category, respect and justice do this on a societal level. Whenever you see "bellies" in the *Tao*, think core values – those beliefs and attitudes that help us contribute to our society, that help us play our part in the whole.

Some translators speak of emptying people's minds or consciousness. Others talk of emptying the citizens' hearts. If we look at the verse from this perspective, we can read "empty hearts" as "reducing emotions". If you make a big deal about exceptions to the rule – life's rarities – be they objects in short supply or "heroes" – you're appealing to people's emotions. Their hearts will generate a jealousy for what they don't have rather than satisfaction with what they do have. As the old World War I song told us, *"How you gonna keep 'em down on the farm after they've seen Paree?"* While the relatively immobile agricultural population of ancient China probably never saw much of the era's large cities and luxuries, the principle remains the same then and now. If you expose someone to something that appears enjoyable and is outside their day-to-day life, you're creating desire, jealousy, frustration and probably a host of other emotions that distract from the task at hand. How many times have you heard a team's coach or manager talk about focusing on this week's game, rather than dreaming of championship rings on their fingers? The wise leader keeps the peace with focus on the here and now; and, as much as possible, by eliminating exposure to the roots of discontent. When you remove these temptations, you're removing a source of distraction and ambition. Sounds a lot like Buddhism, doesn't it? It's one of the many reasons it won easy acceptance when it migrated from India to China.

Another of the *Tao*'s consistent themes, to modestly serve as an example to others, works here. When a leader is "one of us" there really aren't any privileges or objects that create temptation in others. The humble, modest Sage sets an example for others to follow. It's an organic, *Wu-wei* [non-action], approach – not a Confucian hierarchy of rules and regulations. The Sage teaches by example, not by lecture or legislation.

In other words, don't tell me, show me.

- How many times have you put people to sleep with logical, step-by-step instructions, when involving them in a task would have reinforced the lesson, built their enthusiasm and created a buy-in that only comes from participation?

- Have you ever spent so much time dreaming of the happily-ever-after outcome of something that you never started the task that would have led to it?
- Have you ever spent so much time dreaming of the happily-ever-after outcome of something that you ignored your day-to-day responsibilities? And where scrambling to catch up with yourself put your dream even further from ever being realized?

Verse 5

Heaven and earth are impartial. Don't take sides.

The true Sage recognizes that they – like all of us – are part of the natural world. Just as sunbeams and raindrops fall on everyone and everything, the Sage treats everyone equally, without playing favourites. In several places you'll see the *Tao* refer to the Sage as "Not kind". This simply means that the Sage deals from logic, not emotion. Just like the sky that doesn't own the rain but merely lets it flow through, the Sage doesn't own things, but acts simply as a channeling conduit [or, in some translations, as a bellows] bringing things to those in need. Because Sages aren't giving anything that they personally own, there's no need to take credit for being a channel, or even for being modest. And many times people are like kids in a candy shop. They really don't care about the source of things. Don't waste your time, energy or emotions looking for gratitude that most likely will never come in your direction.

Don't let your emotions get in the way of doing what's right and treating everyone equally. There are times when "helping" someone or something on their way actually harms them. There's an oft-told tale of a person helping an emerging butterfly break free of its cocoon. The butterfly died soon after, well before its time. Since it never developed the strength it needed to break its cocoon, it didn't have strength to deal with the outside world. On a personal note, during my lifeguarding days I once received criticism for letting a poor swimmer struggle as long as he did to reach the float on a lake. Yes, I would have jumped in to save him if he'd been drowning. Instead, I gave him time to recover from his exhaustion on the float, reflecting on his limits. Then I helped him back and gave him suitable instructions. If I'd stopped his efforts too early, he might have thought he could have swum further – and put himself in serious danger at a point when there wasn't anyone around to help.

- How many times have you stepped in to help someone – and prevented them from learning? Think of specific instances.
- And how many times have you resented someone else trying to "help" you? Can you create a list of at least five occasions? OK, now go back to the previous question. Can you add at least five more instances to your list?
- What can you do to remedy similar situations in the future? What will you do differently?

Verse 7

The Sage puts himself last, and finds himself in front.

You may be familiar with the phrase, "Living in the world, but not of it." While it usually describes a person single-mindedly devoted to an activity to the exclusion of nearly everything else, it implies that human activity is all that makes up "the world." If this is your perspective, it sounds like you've limited yourself to living in the man-made world, be it material or social. But if you listen to your inner Sage you don't have to abandon this world, just keep it in perspective. It's part of the entire world. Beavers build dams. Coral polyps build reefs. Waves crash and birds sing. If you make some quality time in your life to pay attention to the natural world around us, you might become a bit more aware of humanity's place in creation.

When I say quality time, I mean the time that exists after that mouse treadmill in your brain finally forgets thoughts of work and all the day-to-day tasks that we deem so important to living in the material world. We both know that this last suggestion is harder than it looks. But believe me, it's worth trying. If you've ever spent any time around yoga classes you've probably heard the truism that most people use *savasana,* the final, relaxing pose in most yoga classes, not to relax, but to review that mental checklist of everything else in their over-scheduled day.

Can you get away from it all? Yes. First, find a practice. Then stick with it. It doesn't have to be meditation or yoga. In fact, if it's outdoors in the wind and rain with dirt between your toes instead of on your shoes it might be even more helpful.

After a while you'll find that when we look after the natural world, we're looking out for ourselves. When we only look out for our flesh-and-blood or job-defined self we're ignoring a large part of our being. Imagine your lungs only looking out for the air they use, ignoring the requirements of the rest of the body. How long would they – or you – last?

The sky, sun, moon, trees and water are all part of nature. Sages know we exist as one of them, living just as they do, supporting others without discrimination. [The bones of our rib cage protect our heart, lungs and stomach, which in turn ensure that the bones get their nutrients.] The light of the sun and moon fall on all, as do the falling rain and snow. Sages don't live for themselves. Like the earth and sky – like the universe – like *Tao*, they simply exist.

When we consider ourselves as an individual – a self – we limit our being to whatever fits inside our package of flesh and bone. This self is limited. A person defining themselves as separate draws a line between themselves and creation, the whole of life. The world becomes an object for them to manipulate, not an extension of themselves to nurture and care for. And even if you've never paid much attention to the birds and the bees of the natural world, give some thought to the sports cliché – There's no "I" in Team. Nature's team is considerably larger and more talented than any sports team.

Think for a moment of the word selfish. What's its meaning? What's its root? A related word, ego, is also the root word for egotism in English and several romance languages. [It's OK to take a break here to wander through your translation software to see for yourself. If you want to have some fun and learn something at the same time, type in "selfish" as the English word. Then notice the "ego" root word in nearly every Romance or Germanic European language.]

Self dies. *Tao* doesn't. And the Sage doesn't play favourites.

The Sage lives as an example to others. If being an example is leadership, then in this case it's leadership from behind. Those in front know the source of their strength. You don't have to have a title to be a leader. Know your place. There's no need to advertise yourself. If others want to recognize you, let them. If others want to ignore you, let them.

Or, as modern philosopher Thomas Berry put it in many talks, as well as his book, *Evening Thoughts*: "The universe is composed of subjects to be communed with, not objects to be exploited. Everything has its own voice. Thunder and lightning and stars and planets, flowers, birds, animals, trees – all these have voices, and they constitute the community of existence that is profoundly related."

Learn how to listen. To everyone and everything, no matter their form. How? Go lay on a beach. Sit by some flowers or under a tree. Watch some little kids playing. Don't analyze anything. Just listen. And feel.

And in *Tao*: *No self-interest? Self is fulfilled.* Look beyond your body to fulfill your being.
Here's where you might want to take out a notepad –

- Think of specific times when people haven't let you finish your thought or your project. Was the problem their agenda or your failure to communicate?
- And what about the times when the shoe's been on the other foot. How could you have helped that other person communicate and still achieved your own goal?
- Think of specific events and particular people. We want to look at real life – your own real life – and not examples from some seminar or textbook.
- Now go back to each of your answers here and ask yourself, "What was my point of view?" Were you examining the issue and participating in life at the time as a flesh-and-blood limited self? Or as part of a greater existence, where the two of you are equal beings, even if you're playing different roles?

Verse 12

A Sage provides for the belly. Not the eye.

Too many choices can be confusing. Add ignorance and things can be even worse. Think of kids at a candy counter, ignoring the fruits, vegetables and grains less than an aisle away. Or voters enthralled by promises, never asking how they'll be fulfilled. Or the sheer volume of unsorted, uncategorized information that assaults us nearly every waking minute of every day.

The Sage is content with simplicity, looking for substance instead of the superficial. And the difference between the substance and the superficial? Think of those who scan and react to social media headlines versus those who read and respond because they've discovered that headlines in both new and old media have always been click-bait designed to attract attention, rather than inform. To borrow a line from Shakespeare's *Merchant of Venice*, "All that glisters is not gold." He said essentially the same thing in *Henry VIII*, "All hoods do not make monks". These thoughts have come down to us today in the form of "Beauty is only skin deep."

In *Tao*, taking care of the belly means relying on core values, or staying centered on what really counts in life. Relying on eyes leads to enslavement by the clutter of our manmade environment.

Antoine de St. Exupery's *Little Prince* expressed the same thought, using similar imagery: "It is only with the heart that one can see rightly; what is essential is invisible to the eye."

The Sage not only understands, but feels, priorities.

- When was the last time you actually listened while someone was venting?
- Were you able to help them by simply being there?
- Or did you find a way to gently address their core problem?
- And when was the last time someone was able to help you while you were rambling on about everything in your life?
- How did they do it – what technique did they use?

Verse 22

Want to become whole? Become broken.

Most of us learn from our mistakes. With a little bit of luck, we're lifelong learners because we're constantly exploring what's new to us. Hopefully you'll encounter mentors and guides who'll give you enough freedom to fail gently. And enough support for you to learn thoroughly. And also, hopefully, you'll be flexible enough to adjust your path in light of your experience. *Tao* recognizes that perfection doesn't exist, but that there's a path in perfection's direction. Want to avoid stubbing your toe on life's path? Just refuse to move. Stay stuck in the same place.

Is it possible for the Sage to forego life's clutter on the way to knowledge? Here we're re-emphasizing the appeal to modesty and humility we've seen in Verses 1 and 3. If you're not concerned with making yourself look good, you can devote your time and energy to learning. [There's a certain amount of humility involved in learning, an admission that we don't know everything.] When the world worships artifice and everyone is wrapping themselves in bright bling, those who remain true to their core being and don't chase the crowd are the ones who stand out. Eventually this humility and modesty are noticed, with the Sage as an example to all those tiring of the chase for fashion – until modesty becomes the fashion. Is the Sage who becomes a fashion leader still a sage? [Think of the "gurus" from the East making financial killings in the West.]

Flexibility is key. There's a quote attributed to Thomas Jefferson [although there are no records of him ever saying it], that seems appropriate here: "In matters of principle, stand like a rock. In matters of taste, go with the current." Adjust your sails to the wind, but don't lose sight of your goal.

The Sage's principle of humility, of blending in with the crowd, has found itself embodied in many cultures. Two aphorisms in particular reflect this, seen variously in collections of Chinese, Japanese and Korean proverbs. The tallest flower in the field is picked, leaving the rest to survive. The straightest tree is chopped, leaving the rest – the crooked ones – to grow and reproduce.

You may have heard the old story about the farmer who had a single old horse that helped him work his fields, take him to market and carry his burdens. When the horse ran away all the neighbors consoled him because of his bad luck. "Bad luck, good luck, who knows?" said the farmer. The next week the horse returned, bringing three young wild horses to stay. The neighbors congratulated him on his good luck. "Bad luck, good luck, who knows?" said the farmer.

The farmer's son tried to ride one of the new horses, was thrown and broke his leg. "Bad luck," cried the neighbors. "Bad luck, good luck, who knows?" said the farmer. The next day the army came to take all of the village's able-bodied young men to fight in the Emperor's new war, leaving the farmer's lame son. "Good luck," said the neighbors. "Bad luck, good luck, who knows?" said the farmer.

While the boy healed with but a slight limp, all of the village's other sons died in the war, leaving the farmer and his son as the only ones able to work the fields, making them the wealthiest in the village.

Everyone looked up to them, congratulating them on their good luck. "Bad luck, good luck, who knows?" said the farmer.

The next day the Emperor's tax collector came to town…

- When was the last time you actually set aside time to think? About your life, your goals, and possible ways to eliminate – or at least deal with – some of that chaos surrounding most of us?
- When was the last time you reflected on the lessons you've learned from good times and bad?
- And when are you going to start applying the first of these lessons? After that you can schedule another, and another…

Verse 26

Travel and explore. But don't leave your values behind.

This verse re-states Verse 12. When we accept our abilities – our strengths and weaknesses – we're free in this world. No need to worry about what's not there. We simply appreciate what we have. No matter where we travel, physically, mentally, emotionally or spiritually, we still have our core being, or as *Tao* says it, our provision cart. This baggage is who we are – our core values, our physical attributes – in a sense, these constitute our power base, the places where we have our strength, our confidence.

Have you ever looked out at a beautiful beach or landscape and just felt good about it? Or left an event or person with a calm satisfaction that's beyond words? That's when you're in *Tao*. Most of us have seen exuberant children gleefully opening presents while their parents look on in calm appreciation. This calmness comes with maturity's wisdom.

If your tastes run more to competitive sports, you may be familiar with Lou Holtz, the American football coach. One day an interviewer asked him why his players never celebrated in the end zone after scoring a touchdown. His reply? "I want them to act like they've been there before."

If Christmas mornings or competitive sports aren't your thing, here's an old story told by Zen master Soen-roshi:

One day a young monk went with his teacher on a long hike up Mount Fuji. Although the young monk had seen Fuji many times before, this time he truly felt himself as being in oneness with the mountain and all it embodied. All along the trail he kept exclaiming over the wildflowers, birds, the reflected light in the trees, and the sacred mountain's magnificent silence and more. In his excitement he asked his teacher if he saw the same things. "Yes," said the old monk, "but isn't it a pity to say so."

The Sage, being part of nature, accepts the world as it is. Simply put, be consistent. Keep to your path and don't be distracted. Appreciate beauty – and ugliness as well – because we can't have one without recognizing the other.

- Do you take the time to look at snowflakes as things of beauty – instead of slippery barriers to wherever you think you need to be? What about their cousin, a foggy, misty morning?
- In your head – or on a piece of paper – make a list of the things in your life that have become part of that personal wallpaper you ignore as background in your over-full life, when they're really beautiful murals that deserve some attention.

Verse 27

The good man teaches the bad. The bad man is a lesson for the good.

What's good? What does it take to be good?

Verse 27 starts with a series of examples. Like many speakers with general audiences, The *Tao* uses the same example, repeating it several times, each time in a different way. Good traveling/bookkeeping/knot-tying and so forth are simply ways of flowing with *Tao* – being a part of the planet, not apart from it, socially as well as physically.

The Sage's modesty allows teaching and caring for others without the ego or need for recognition getting in the way. Leaving no tracks or trace is simply being humble – allowing the task and others to come first. Life is a two-way transaction – teachers and students need each other. Everyone and everything in the world has a purpose.

You'll find modesty and humility as recurring themes in *Tao*. While we're all part of nature, the Sage recognizes that they may just be a bug on a leaf on a tree in a forest on an island in a lake in another forest. No matter how beautiful and inspirational they may be to others, they recognize their bughood or leafhood, knowing that at some point they'll fall from their branch to become compost for others.

Oh, and I'll admit that one part of this verse confused me for a while. If you read this verse in your own copy of the *Tao Te Ching*, you'll see the phrase, "no one can untie it". I wondered about it. I stared at my pile of reference books, not really wanting to start digging through them. Then the light bulb turned on. Once you've taught something – or learned something – it can't be undone. When you recognize this part of your Sagehood, be careful about what you say and do. You don't want to fill up your world – and everyone else's world – with junk.

And finally, we all need to remember that we teach by example. Hopefully we're good examples for others, and not examples of how not to be. Or, as Oscar Wilde told us in *The Duchess of Padua*, "Some cause happiness wherever they go; others whenever they go." [He "borrowed" the thought from Shakespeare's *1 Henry VI*]

- When was the last time someone "put you in your place"?
- Can you see your position from their point of view?
- Could you have handled the situation better, maybe even creating a win-win situation?

Verse 29

Trying to control the world? It probably can't be done.

Are you holding on to something with all your might? This sort of defeats the purpose of owning it, doesn't it? How can you use it? Holding on to people or things keeps them from being themselves, from fulfilling their function in their own lives as well as ours. Think of the New Age poster that permeates shops and social media: "If you love someone let them go. If they return, they're yours. If they don't, they never were." Or of all the business and biblical axioms contrasting those who hide their riches under beds with those who invest and put them to work.

We all have our strengths and weaknesses. When we recognize this in ourselves, we're comfortable surrounding ourselves with people who [1] can compensate for our own weaknesses and [2] benefit from our strengths.

Look at the world of nature...

Different plants have different functions – some provide our food, others our building materials, still others provide good environments for local plants and animals. People are the same.

I used to re-hab old houses. Can I install the plumbing and electrics? Yes. Do I have pride in my work? Yes. Would the building inspector pass the jobs? Yes. But there are people who can do these jobs better and faster than me, so I hired them so that I could do things I'm more skilled at. Doesn't it make sense to let the athletes, bakers, carpenters, doctors and everyone else do what they're good at and hopefully love?

Seasons change, bringing different approaches and different needs. As we're told in *Ecclesiastes 3:1-8* and the Pete Seeger song, *Turn, Turn, Turn*, to everything there is a season. Whether it's sports, building construction or family holiday planning, we've learned to pay attention to Mother Nature's seasons.

So, you see, you're already well on the way to being a Sage. You can respect the currents of nature as well as the attributes of its citizens. You can tamper with Mother Nature and kill the goose that lays golden eggs, or you can work within the world, serving as an example for others.

Part of non-action is letting nature take its course.

- Think of the last time someone disagreed with you. Did you respect their perspective?
- Did the situation allow for discussion? Were you able to show them a better way?
- If not, were they able to show you how their way was better – and have you been able to begin building a relationship for a better future? How?

Verse 47

Observe the world. But don't abandon yourself or your roots.

Wise people don't get caught up in the minutiae of everyday life.

We can look out our window or door to see and feel what's happening in a single glance – or we can focus on a single item like a speck on the glass and miss the big picture. It's that feeling – something's good or something's wrong – that we need to pay attention to. The Sage listens to their heart with their heart, hearing that voice that doesn't use words but speaks more clearly than thousands of books. Remember what the Little Prince told us: *"It is only with the heart that one can see rightly; what is essential is invisible to the eye."*

You may also recall Einstein's observation that problems can't be solved at the same level that created them. Monks, hermits and other recluses throughout history withdrew from the everyday world for many reasons. One of these was the perspective that comes from looking within ["without opening your door"]. This doesn't mean becoming a bookworm and shutting out the outside world, rather it's a lesson in priorities. Since we're all part of the one, recognize the role you're playing on this planet. When we get a full night's sleep, we see our world with a new set of eyes. Look at holidays, retreats and other withdrawals from daily chaos in the same way. You'll not only recharge your battery but you'll re-focus your inner eyes, as well.

Verse 47 continues, "The more you experience, the less you know". If you're filling your mind with images of the world around you, there's a good chance you're ignoring their common source, ourselves. They, like us, are part of the universe. If you're focused on a bug on a leaf, you may not realize that you're living in a forest. You've probably heard the phrase describing an expert as one who knows more and more about less and less, until they know everything there is to know about absolutely nothing. Those relying to an undue degree on algorithm-driven social media, in particular, can find themselves addicted, exhausted and suffering from a limited worldview that's divorced from actual experience in the physical world.

The Sage can know without going this far – people are pretty much the same wherever we go. Situations change. Don't get smothered in the non-essentials of a situation. It's more important to address causes than symptoms.

We know that it's hard to remember that your mission is to empty the swamp if you're up to your ass in alligators. Have you considered that your mission may be ill-advised in the first place? Or that there might be a better way of accomplishing your task if you're not in the middle of it?

When you let nature take its course, you'll find yourself preferring substance over style.

- When was the last time you took the time to look at something you've completed – and realized that either [a] it never needed doing or [b] there were lots of easier ways of doing it?

- How many times in the past year have you actually done this review?
- What will you need to do with your life to turn this review process into a preview task?

Verse 49

The Sage's mind is empty, waiting to be filled by the minds of others.

We're all one – so why dislike or distrust part of yourself? If something's bothering you, find its cause and address it if you can. Accept it if you can't. Do you cut off your arm because it itches? Take out your eye because you don't have whatever we define as "perfect" vision? Or because you don't care for what you're seeing? Of course not. Other people are part of us and we're part of them. Life's a lot simpler when we treat everyone with respect.

We all use shortcuts to simplify life. A word or a name describes something or somebody simply. There's a use for this. When I tell you a Category 5 hurricane is coming, my expectation is that you'll begin to take appropriate precautions because you understand what a hurricane is. If I told you that an oceanic low-pressure system was approaching with high sustained winds, you may dismiss my comment as an interesting but insignificant academic factoid. My knowledge of meteorology can help me give specific advice regarding the best precautions to take. My knowledge of communications – or my contact with communicators – lets me do so effectively.

The Sage is open-minded, treating all like their own family, recognizing that each has different wants, needs and abilities. A key characteristic of being open minded is an ability to avoid preconceived notions, to listen carefully to what people mean as well as what they're saying. Preconceived notions limit our vision

– they put blinders on us and restrict our path. Different people say the same thing in different ways. They may also hear us in their own ways, filtering our words through their own filters. So…when we respond to them it often means telling the same story, giving the same lesson, in several different ways. Flexibility of communication doesn't mean sacrificing consistency in message.

A sage recognizes life's flow and uses this knowledge to create harmony. There are times when we need to recognize that unpleasant people or situations carry important messages for us. Be sure to thank them.

The sage is a selfless role model, remembering to let others take credit for things since we're all one and it really doesn't make much difference. When a hand holds something, does it matter which finger says it's essential?

- Have you ever discovered that your initial judgement about another person was wrong?
- How did you handle it when you discovered you underestimated – or overestimated – them?
- What did you do when you found that someone wasn't as good as you initially thought?

Verse 57

Win the world with non-action.

This is one of those verses where sage and leader are sometimes conflated. We generally look to leaders to "do something" – while it's the Sage who counsels thought and non-action.

Many people – particularly in the West – feel an urge to "take action". And if they're in a position of power or control, to not only do something, but to stamp their name on it. It's the ego. It's something we've come to recognize – almost to the point of acceptance. If we elect leaders or representatives, it's to do something new or to undo something a previous leader did. Whether we're talking of political leaders or business magnates, the impulse is the same. Most prefer to look at the past and re-make it in their own manner. A few of the advanced ones look to their personal vision of the future and re-make their domains to match this vision. But if they're too far ahead of their people, they'll incur wrath rather than welcome. Smart visionaries know that lasting change has evolutionary roots, not revolutionary ones. Coffee plants can't grow in lava, but thrive in the volcanic soil that eventually appears from lava, years after the eruption.

Those looking to the past are like generals who look to their own experience in fighting their most recent war. They'll usually be beaten by the next generation, who understands the current environment and uses contemporary tools and tactics. And if you think this example only applies to war and politics, consider the story of Ingvar Kamprad, a 23-year-old Swede who had to remove the legs from a table to fit it into his car. Until that point, he'd never thought much about furniture. He then created IKEA. Using today's hindsight, the concept is simple. But it's an approach that traditional, experienced and expert furniture manufacturers and retailers had never considered.

Since Kamprad had never been taught the accepted ways of doing things, he didn't know what couldn't be done.

As we look at the tools of those who rule our world and run our economies – taboos, weapons, laws and more – we also need to recognize that these actions and attempts to impose behaviour on society simply create reactions. Just as in any other field, action creates reaction. The Confucianism of its day used rules and regulations and found it created conflict rather than the stasis it desired. The second part of this verse lists the causes of society's problems. Their common thread? Force. This appears to be a direct slap at Confucian philosophy and practice. The solution? *Tao*'s non-action. "I do nothing…"

Consider the forest fire. Is it good or bad? From the point of view of many people, it's bad, because it burns towns and destroys the homes people build in the forest. But from the forest's point of view, it clears brush, encourages certain seeds to germinate and allows the forest to renew itself.

And when it's renewed, men can continue using it. Do you listen to those with short-term or long-term views?

- When was the last time you ignored, or found a way around, a process you disagreed with? [You mean you've never

ignored a traffic signal or taken advantage of an unintended loophole to do something counter to a rule's intent?]
- Have you ever decided not to correct someone else's error because the issue just wasn't that important and you didn't want to ruin the relationship?
- How have you reacted when you've been caught breaking a law, rule or taboo?
- What have you done when somebody shows how you're mistaken in response to your telling them something they believe is wrong?

Verse 58

If a ruler is humble, people can become whole. If a ruler is repressive, people learn treachery.

Verse 58 continues the thoughts of 57, pointing out the problems inherent in a Confucian "law and order" society and reinforcing *Tao*'s view of opposites, or complementarity.

For the most part, if we treat people with respect, it will be returned. Consider the plight of the customer service person on a help desk. Their only public contact is with people who are frustrated and angry over a product's problems – and that's before spending way-too-much time with automated menus and saccharine music. [*"Due to temporary high call volumes, your wait time may be absurdly long"* simply means that the firm refuses to hire more reps.] Many companies have a love and leave 'em approach when it comes to sales and service. I've had just as many product problems as the next person, but I've found that they're usually resolved quickly on the first call because I treat the phone rep with respect, using a sense of humor about the entire situation. If we can help to make that stressed person comfortable, they may find it easier to resolve our particular issue.

While today's web-linked society may differ from ancient China's, people's basic personalities remain pretty much the same. Accepting the fact that there is a given percentage of society that will try to scam the system, what's the best way to deal with it? Should we build checkpoints and procedures into every part of government and society to prevent fraud? But this harms business and frustrates everyday honest citizens who are just trying to live their lives. Should we streamline life so that it's easy to do things? Then the scam artists will prosper. At what point does the cost of regulation exceed the cost of corruption?

- When was the last time you used politeness and respect to mitigate a stressful encounter?
- When did someone calm your anger or frustration with their behaviour?
- What can you do in your own life to cultivate good relations with everyone you meet, not just your friends?

Verse 60

Rule in accord with Tao. Spirits lose their power.

Continuing the thoughts of several preceding verses, we're again conflating the Sage and the ruler while believing in the basic decency of most people. As with other professions, the Sage/ruler should, first of all, do no harm.

Are these spirits [sometimes translated as demons and ghosts] non-human – or simply bad rulers? If we take the first view, we're taking Taoism back to its Shamanic roots. Either way, we're contrasting Taoistic laissez-faire with Confucian regulated behaviour. If you rule in the spirit of *Tao*, neither your ancestors' spirits nor today's humans will have anything to bother you about. We can all live peacefully in our own worlds, not bothering others, be they spiritual or physical.

When we rule our personal world with *Tao*, we don't contrive. Things beyond our control occur naturally, so we need to expect the unexpected and anticipate potential problems before they become actual problems. If we maintain an awareness of our environment, we'll be in a position to deal with natural change without having to play catch-up. The Sage suggests that we don't build our homes on sandy beaches [*Matthew 7:26*]. The materialist, rarely looking beyond their next bank deposit, builds in the path of a hurricane and looks for compliments on how well they recovered from the disaster when they used other people's money.

The key here is to encourage and maintain harmony – what's the best way to do this? Live in harmony with our earth's forces. And in the human world, create harmonious conditions. Don't micromanage. As most of today's management consultants and motivational speakers would put it, "Get good people. Then get out of their way."

- How did you show respect to each one of the last ten people you encountered?
- How did you help their day?
- How do you wish the last ten people you encountered could have treated you differently?
- What changes will you make in your life to fulfill these wishes?

Verse 63

Act without rushing. Do by not doing what doesn't need doing.

Or, to quote Ben Franklin, an ounce of prevention is worth a pound of cure. [He said it when he was promoting the establishment of Philadelphia's first professional fire company.]

Here *Tao* is simply giving the Sage/leader another application of *Wu-wei*. Think of the number of times you've seen people congratulating each other on how well they dealt with a particular disaster – storm, fire, flood, etc. Contrast this with the Sage who prepares ahead of time – doesn't build on a flood plain, makes sure the roof is sound, has sufficient supplies and so forth.

The Sage views the easy problems of today as the big ones of tomorrow. In effect the Sage deals with the seed, so we can harvest later. By doing a little bit now, without recognition, we can avoid the need for a lot of work later. Of course, if your goal is public recognition and not modest invisibility, wait until after the disaster. Then show up with a lot of relief aid, media in tow. Hopefully the press will thank you for dealing with disaster without asking about the preparation you should have encouraged.

When you've been injured or insulted by someone else, how do you deal with it?

Do you react and repay them in kind? You may recall the statement that Gandhi never said, "An eye for an eye makes the whole world blind."

Or do you respond, defusing the immediate action [if possible] and addressing its cause. It's part of most people's nature to help those who are kind to us. If we treat everyone as a friend and equal, life can be a lot easier, even if you create a bit of confusion among those who feel that they want to harm you. This approach isn't unique to *Tao*. We find it in the more recent past in Jesus' advice to "do unto others as you would have them do unto you." [*Matthew 7:12, Luke 6:31*]

- When was the last time you spent more money than necessary, because you waited until the last minute?
- Are you one of those people who are always last to an event? Do hosts and organizers always give you a starting time that's a half hour earlier than the one they give others?
- What can you do to give more respect to your wallet and to other people, to avoid these situations?

Verse 64

What's at peace is easy to hold. But why hold it?

Verse 64 continues the advice from the previous one, giving us the famous "journey of 1,000 steps/miles" admonition. [The actual distance in the original document is 1,000 *li* – about 500 meters in today's measure. While this is nice-to-know, it doesn't change the basic thought the verse is transmitting.] Life's all in the timing. Start now, while you have the energy – things will go more smoothly. It's easier to tie down your possessions now, before the storm comes, than during it, while you're subject to its winds and rain. Also, look at the seeds of the future – it's better to get out of town now, before the Emperor's men are after you. Or...plant a seed, pour a foundation, clear a path for the plant, building or road you'll want later. Create the conditions for success and you'll find it'll come a lot easier.

Remember that there's often no recognition in preparing the land or planting the seed you've saved from last year. But people will be thankful for the harvest banquet. Whether people recognize your participation in nature's flow or whether they're just ignorant and hungry, doesn't matter as long as their stomachs are filled.

But...life's more than just timing. It's also attitude. If you feel a need to hold on to something for dear life it may be time to question your views on the difference between needs and wants.

Are you wasting your time and energy on non-essentials? If you feel this way about a person, are the feelings being returned? You've no doubt seen the poster adorning many gift shops that also carry the

"1,000 miles" one: "If you love someone set them free. If they come back, they're yours. If they don't, they never were."

Life's about priorities. How will you use your energy?

- Do people who never begin projects until after a deadline passes disrupt your life? Or are you one of those people who disrupt others' lives?
- Do you find yourself spending more time and money fixing and correcting problems in things that were done quickly and cheaply – or are you proud of how fast and cheaply you work? Remember the axiom: Better, Cheaper, or Faster – pick any two because you can't have all three at the same time.
- How can you help others – or yourself – change their habits to create more harmony and respect?

Verse 66

How did the great rivers become great? They are good at keeping low.

Successful leaders position themselves as being from ordinary stock, as being "one of the people." Whether they truly are – or are just successful actors – is another conversation. Whether we're a public leader or simply someone's counselor, we need to establish our credibility, to show that we understand our audience's background and concerns with our hearts and ears as well as our minds.

When rivers flow into the sea, they're going to a lower level. This imagery works on several levels. First is the emotional connection that most of us have with water – tears of love, tears of joy, tears of sadness. Then of course there's the fact that many people see generosity as something that flows, like water, from fullness into emptiness. And then we come back to the source of political and civic power. No matter how exalted your background, success is built on the foundation supplied by "the lowly", the common people.

How do you talk with the people's voice? By listening to them. We have two ears and only one mouth. It's usually a good idea to use them in that 2:1 proportion. The best leaders know how to follow the public opinion they've probably helped to mold.

The key to all this? Not just perceived, but actual humility. A more recent text phrased it as "...so the last will be first and the first last..." [*Matthew 20:16, Mark 10:31, Luke 13:30*]

If you can actually practice this preaching with modesty, you'll find that it helps others. It might even be an example for them on how to act. And if two of you are acting that way, it'll be nice, but may not draw much attention. And if three people do it, people might start noticing and suggesting you create a center. And can you imagine three times three times three people spreading a contagion of helping by listening?

The best leaders don't lead, they inspire.

- How did someone inspire you when you were a child?
- Who gave you a lifelong lesson that you still use today? How did they do it?
- How will you inspire someone today?

Verse 68

The best leaders serve their people.

"There go the people. I must follow them, for I am their leader." While there's no definitive source for this bromide, its first use is generally attributed to Alexandre Ledru-Rollin, a 19th century French revolutionary.

Leading from behind doesn't mean putting your boot up people's butts. It means creating an environment that encourages others to do their best because they want to, not because you're ordering them to.

When you inspire people, you'll do less perspiring and they'll do better work. What's the best way to motivate people? It will come as no surprise that the answer is, "It depends." Think for a moment of *Star Trek*'s two leaders, Kirk and Spock. One led from his heart, the other with his brain. Each had their strengths and weaknesses and the series relied on playing to their strengths, using the leadership quality appropriate to the interplanetary crisis du jour. Those scripts worked with archetypes, using what I tend to call sledgehammer morality. You have the advantage of being able to work with more subtle approaches.

Citizens are not cattle. But if you use the latest knowledge about cattle you might wind up treating people more humanely. Temple Grandin of Colorado State University has won international acclaim for saving money and improving processing time in feedlots by looking at fencing, transport and cattle chutes from the cow's point of view, not man's. Have you ever thought of looking at a task from a worker's point of view, rather than an accountant's? The end result might even make the accountant happy. While there's a place for task- and budget-oriented management by objective [MBO] don't ever forget that it's people and process that underlie a successful MBO program.

As a public leader, you're on a pedestal, open to everyone's view. If people suspect your strength, but never see it demonstrated, there's a good chance they'll over-estimate your power. This is a particularly valuable asset in any type of competition, where your opposite's ignorance can generate either an ineffective conservatism or an even less-effective rashness.

- Can you think of times that an "expert's" attentions actually interfered with the work they expected you to do?
- How would you have handled the situation differently?
- Is this how you handle things when dealing with others who are "beneath" you in a hierarchy – be they children or employees?
- Don't confuse your position in a hierarchy with your role as a human being.

Verse 70

The Tao's words are easy to understand. Easier to practice. Yet no one understands them.

Sure, it's easy to praise verbosely ambitious mission statements and lofty goals, but how many of us actually make the time to practice what we preach? How many of us talk to be understood, rather than impress others with our vocabulary?

And how many of us simply pay attention to the styles and rituals of life without learning or practicing their substance? Whether it's following the interpreted or misinterpreted teachings of our religion's founder, or actually working with the goals and objectives of that business plan we prepared for the bankers, it's a rare person who walks the walk and talks the talk.

Life has changed since those days in ancient China. In many ways it's harder for us to follow these precepts. How many times have you simply scanned and reacted to something you've seen on social media, rather than actually reading and responding to it? Or just ignored social media for a few days in favor of more worthwhile things? Today's life is busy and multi-layered. If we can deal with a symptom and move on to our next task, we feel we've accomplished something. But many times, that symptom is a side-effect, and not the cause of our problem. It takes more time to return to an issue several times than it would have taken to study and solve its cause. Even if we're adults, the time pressures we place on ourselves take us back to childhood days, searching for candy-shop satisfaction without a thought of nutrition, much less sugar crashes, calories and cavities.

Oh, and that "no one can understand" part of the verse? It simply means practice what you preach. If you don't follow *Tao,* it's impossible for you to practice its teaching. The words have ancestors – they have meaning. Deeds have masters – we're dealing with both the concept of action and non-action as well as master/subject vs. a person who's a humble example to others. Things and people aren't always what they appear to be on first glance. Is the most influential person the one in public office or the humble man in everyday garb? The business boss or the gatekeeper receptionist? [My kingdom is not of this world – *John 18:36*]

- When was the last time somebody politely put you off, only to get bitten later by an issue you were raising?
- When was the last time you ignored or deferred action on a little issue, only to see it come back as a big issue later?
- Recognizing that there's not enough time in most days to slow down for everything, how can you change your decision-making process – or decision-delegating process – to replace a reactive environment with a predictive, responsive one?

Verse 71

Knowing you don't know makes you whole.
Thinking you know it all is a disease.

How many times have you heard someone start a conversation with, "I don't know much about - - - - ", and then proceed to demonstrate how little they know? There's a comment often attributed to Mark Twain, stating that it's better to remain silent and be thought a fool than to open your mouth and remove all doubt.

Verse 71 simply continues the thoughts of Verse 70, promoting wisdom and humility as important attributes of a Sage.

A more recent view of *Tao*'s recognition of our limits is found in 1999's Dunning-Kruger study entitled, "Unskilled and Unaware of It: How Difficulties in Recognizing One's Own Incompetence Lead to Inflated Self-Assessments." In brief, it tells us that the ignorant don't know they're ignorant. They're over-confident because they're unaware of the fact that there may be things they know nothing about. In more popular jargon – and contemporary politics – we can lift a line from Alexander Pope's "*Essay on Criticism*": "Fools rush in where angels fear to tread."

- When was the last time you just nodded in agreement when you had no idea what someone was talking about?
- When you recognize that you're over your head in something, do you make the time to go back to basics and learn what you need to learn? Do you ask for help?
- Or do you just plow through and hope for the best?

Verse 72

When people no longer fear your power…

If you're the boss, do you want people's fear or their respect? Slavish followers? Or enthusiastic co-workers contributing to the cause you all share? If you're their Sage – their advisor – should they follow you by rote with fear or with understanding and love? Worse than this is creating an atmosphere of rebellion, where people who feel they have nothing more to lose rise up against you.

Life's ideal lies in doing things because we want to, not because we have to. And this ideal is easier for all to fulfill when people understand you from their hearts, not their heads. It doesn't matter what sport you follow, or even if you don't follow any at all. Nearly all of us have seen clips of powerful locker room speeches that unite and motivate a team, creating a winning attitude – and more importantly in a sports environment, that burst of adrenaline that helps their common quest for victory.

As in many previous verses, *Tao* encourages the Sage to practice humility and non-action to achieve this. In today's business parlance, we encourage managers to hire the best, and let them do their job without interference. In agricultural parlance that worked for Lao Tzu as well as for today, create good conditions for good seed, giving encouragement and guidance only when it's needed. See which way a tree is growing before you stake it.

Mother, but don't smother.

- Do you praise and thank people in specific terms, or just in a pro-forma greeting card way?
- Do you thank people on a regular basis – or at all?
- How do you feel when you've given your all to a project and see someone else get credit for it?

Verse 73

Over-confidence is deadly.

Courage takes many forms. But what's courage? Is it an adrenaline-fueled charge into combat or the public disagreement with those who want to shoot first and ask questions later? What are the impossible odds that courage fights? Are they countless opponents driving us to action – or are they the people on our own side who refuse to consider more thoughtful options?

Many times we need courage to have the generosity and patience praised in the previous verse, Verse 72. It's a courage that requires going against the grain, which in most cases is the courage to practice non-action in the face of a society that seems to demand action at every breath and every step along the way.

And if you choose not to go with the flow toward action? Yes, there are consequences. Several cultures tell tales of the straightest tree or the most beautiful flower being stolen from its natural home to be killed and used for the purposes of the few, not for all. What's left for species reproduction? The weak and crooked. [But if most emulate the tallest and most beautiful. . .]

But – and this requires the wisdom of the Sage – we should remember the lessons of ju-jitsu, which is to engage your opponent, but to practice non-action, using their own strength against them. When the time is right, you let your opponent's momentum carry them to defeat. Champion boxer Muhammad Ali stood tall against the forces of politics and racism. He suffered for it. Years later people praised him for his integrity. Sages are human, too. They must recognize their own strengths and weaknesses and choose their battles accordingly.

Dealing with childish demands for something you know is bad may be difficult, but it's doable. I recognize that when these demands come from childish people in adult bodies that it's even more difficult. But it's still doable.

- How have you handled unreasonable demands from your peers?
- How have you handled unreasonable demands from people you think should know better?
- In each case, how could you have handled the situation more effectively? Remember that you probably can't control others, but you can control yourself.

Verse 77

Heaven's way takes from those with too much and gives to those in need. Man has a different way.

Nature is self-regulating. In fact, the "balance of nature" is a phrase that many of us hear quite often. Water finds its own level. Stressing part of a branch – or a muscle – releases the tension in a complementary place.

Humans, however, seem to have lost this intuitive ability somewhere along the way. Balance is no longer assumed, it needs to be taught. Those living as part of nature, like the Sage, practice this charitable balance of nature naturally. You've probably read tales of indigenous tribes with minimal contact with the Western world to whom sharing equally comes naturally. The rest of us, centered on our individual humanity rather than our place in nature, need to be taught.

While rarely making direct reference to our place in the natural world, most religions recognize the need for balance. Some appeal to our individual sense of desire or greed, others to a need for justice.

- Christ is quoted as telling the rich man that the way to heaven is to sell all he has and give to the poor. [*Matthew 19:21, Mark, 10:21, Luke 12:33*]
- One of the Five Pillars of Islam is Zakat, charity to those with less.

- Within Judaism, Maimonides' Eight Levels of Charity says the same thing.
- Hindus practice Seva, selfless service.
- How do you put this into practice in your own life? List some specific examples.
    - With your family?
    - With your social group?
    - In your job?

Verse 78

There is nothing weaker than water...

After World War I France built the Maginot line, an impregnable network of bunkers and forts. German forces simply went around and over them at the beginning of World War II, using tactics and equipment that didn't exist in the first war.

In India, Ireland and the United States, Gandhi, Daniel O'Connell and Martin Luther King used flexible non-violent demonstrations of mass support to wear down their opposition, which was experienced in military and diplomatic combat, but not mass movements with multiple, often uncoordinated, approaches and attack tactics. A key to water's success lies in persistence in the face of resistance as well as its pervasive ability to find and utilize cracks and flaws in its opposition.

Rulers and conquerors recognize opponents like themselves, users of force. Just as generals are renowned for fighting the last war, those who've fought their way to success are often blind to others and their techniques. Grassroots leaders draw their strength from people and ideas rather than politics and powerful weapons. Unless a leader uses the tools of the Sage we've been talking about, their strength will erode and the cliff they've used as a pedestal will become an unstable ledge.

Be it an organic mass movement, guerilla warfare or innovative marketing, it's the antithesis of the Confucian concept of top-down management and rigid adherence to rules. Beyond the peaceful demonstrations mentioned above, consider the guerilla tactics used by colonials versus the British in 18th Century America – or those used by Ho Chi Minh against the Americans in 20th Century Viet Nam. Or consider the effects of the internet age on retailers and media companies who've failed to adapt to changes in consumer habits and preferences.

Let's look beyond politics and warfare to business. In the 1960's multi-purpose spray cleaner *Formula 409* had a comfortable American market niche and almost no competition. When household goods marketing giant Procter & Gamble decided to enter this market, it used all the weight of its Confucian top-down, step-by-step manufacturing and marketing ability. Being a small, closely-held company, *Formula 409* used guerilla tactics by withdrawing its product from P&G's test markets, stopping advertising and refusing to re-fill shelves. Naturally, P&G's *Cinch* had an extremely successful test and began the ponderously massive effort needed for national distribution. In the time that it took P&G to organize itself, *Formula 409* expanded its distribution, cut prices and sold "2 for 1" packages, so that by the time P&G's *Cinch* hit the shelves, nearly every American home that used this type of spray cleaner had more than enough of it in their house. In less than a year, P&G declared defeat and withdrew its product.

P&G was a marketing monolith, but like most monoliths, was inflexible. *Formula 409*'s management, like its product, knew how to exploit the cracks in its opponents' armour.

Successful marketing, warfare, politics and diplomacy are all built on water's strength.

Consider your job. How can you achieve more by doing less?

- What tasks that are done from inertia and tradition really don't fit any more?
- What people are in positions that really don't match their talents?
- How can you reduce interference from ignorant managers – and how can you be respectful to those who may have more perspective than you?

Verse 79

Difficulties linger, even after they're resolved.

It's better to take responsibility than blame. Deal with what you can control, which is rarely others' behaviour and almost never their feelings. Harbouring ill will simply reinforces toxicity within ourselves.

This verse, in a different manner, also demonstrates an issue we've probably all encountered in the world of social media: the written word is easily subject to misinterpretation. Without the nuance expressed through pacing, inflection and body language, it's easy for a statement to be misinterpreted and misunderstood. Irony and sarcasm are among the first victims of social media contact between strangers, quickly followed by detailed analysis of almost anything. Professional translators of *The Tao* make the same point through conflicting interpretations. In ancient China a piece of wood was broken in two, with one half going to a creditor and the other to the debtor. Some versions have the Sage playing the creditor, others the debtor. The right and left halves of the contract also have different meanings. How is this so? The translators, reflecting their own cultural biases and filters, are dealing with glyphs, not sentences which can be parsed. Having said that, even with conflicting translations, the translators keep the same meaning in their work: The Sage promotes peace and agreement, not conflict and blame.

Just be aware that many times people don't mean what they say – because they may not know the meaning of their words. Be human, not a dictionary. Sometimes it's better to be nice than it is to be right, because in the end, justice prevails.

If you haven't done so already, you might want to

- Pick up your copy of the *Tao* and read Verses 76-79 as a single verse.
- Then come back to these thoughts.
- Then write your own version of them.
- And, perhaps, apply them to your own life.

Verse 81

True words may not sound beautiful, beautiful sounding words may not be true.

Tao's final verse: The summary of a lesson? Or an invitation to start the cycle again?

A car dealer's words will talk about the beautiful car that you'll want to drive home. Your mechanic will probably be more honest, telling you things the salesperson would prefer you never learn til it's too late.

"You can't tell a book by its cover." We've heard this many times before, in many different versions. But how many of us take the time to actually open that book, read it and learn from it? Are we so focused on the next item in our to-do list that we glance at a person, situation or event – taking them at the shorthand of face value, which may hide their true benefit or hazard to us? Unless we recognize the meaning of the symptom, we'll most likely spend more time and money dealing with the aftermath of a problem than we would have spent dealing with its source.

So, where do you get the best return on your investment in time – by scanning or studying?

In today's over-stimulated world, it's not easy to spend time researching and learning about everything that affects us. But we have access to other eyes, other senses. They're called other people. Teamwork doesn't mean giving up your identity, it means contributing your strength to a common goal that you share with others. Cooperation yields more benefits than competition. When we give our best to the group, our return is greater than if we kept it to ourselves. Does wealth of anything come from hoarding our resources or putting them out there to work with others?

It doesn't matter whether you've barely scanned or deeply studied this book's comments. Here's your test, to be graded by only yourself:

- List the three most important lessons you've learned from these comments.
- In no more than one sentence for each of these three, say how you'll make them part of your life.
- Set a deadline to achieve each one, listing steps if needed.
- Take a break. You don't need to do everything by yesterday. In fact, you may not need to "do" anything at all, if you just adjust your attitude…

The Sage

Te – an introduction

One of the most common interpretations of *Te* is to call it virtue. But what's virtue? The answer, as we've come to understand with many things in the *Tao Te Ching*, is "it depends."

In this context, we can generally say that virtue is a characteristic of a person who becomes one with the Way. How do we identify this person? And how do we use words to define The Way? That's what this chapter is about.

Before we get started on *Te*, a few notes on this significant part of the *Tao Te Ching*.

If you begin an online search, you'll find well over 100 English translations and interpretations of the *Tao Te Ching*. There are other excellent ones that have never been placed online. All were created with varying degrees of skill and purpose, aimed at different audiences. Most of the major public domain versions use their authors' widely varying editorial judgements in describing *Te*. More recent versions return to old texts, either adding commentary or letting readers make their own decisions.

Now that we've got that out of the way, how do we translate the symbol for *Te*?

美德 In the *Tao Te Ching*, *Te* is usually written as a composite of two characters, with the first one, preceding *Te/virtue*, meaning beautiful or nice.

So here's our exercise, along with a few starter definitions. We're going to work with *Tao's* verse 38, which contrasts *Te* with the Confucian rituals of its day. In fact, it could be called the document's most anti-Confucian verse. The unthinking practice of ancient – but now meaningless – rituals really hasn't changed much from then to now.

First, I've replaced the archaic and academic translations you'll find in many books with a more contemporary one. Then it'll be your turn to create your personal *Tao*, your personal path. Whether it's from your own knowledge, what you find in this essay, in another translation, or from a thesaurus or dictionary, replace my suggested word with one of your own. Then read the verse again.

Does it make sense to you? Great. Think about the steps you can take to incorporate your *Tao* into your everyday life, to make your life a reflection of your *Tao*. And if doesn't make sense to you? Then work with it some more.

Te, or virtue

To help you make some sense of the exercise, we'll first look at the verse's structure. If you remember that *Tao's* roots spring from older, oral, traditions, you'll recognize its point/counterpoint pattern, one that makes it easy to recite, easy to remember. This verse begins by recognizing *Te* in its highest form, creating a contrast with its next lowest form. As you read or recite the following verse, you'll see that the "next lowest" is compared to an even lower form of *Te*, and so on until we reach full Confucian ritual for its own sake without any meaning or love. To qualify different levels of *Te*, you'll also see the use and misuse of *Wu-wei*, or non-action.

So…as you replace these words with your own, you'll see the progression from a state of being for its own sake to a state of doing because you feel that outside forces demand it of you. Your motivation is reflected in your action or non-action.

Here's the progression, using words you may find in various translations.

道 ***Tao*** – path

德 ***Te*** – the nature of one who follows the path, usually translated as virtue. Sometimes shown as a single glyph, as here. Other times with two characters, as above.

仁 ***Ren*** – universal humanity, virtue, kind heartedness, benevolence. On a higher level, this can be a form of *Te*.

义 **Yi** – group righteousness, not universal humanity, but localized or tribal. The organized, structured, approved social constructs that we use to "fit in".

礼 **Li** – propriety. Doing something because it's expected of us, without understanding its reason or meaning. Think of ritual for the sake of ritual, not its original intrinsic meaning. [Like focusing on the finger, rather than the goal it's pointing to, because everyone around you is admiring their own fingers.]

Let's also look at *Tao's* use of "high" and "low". Are they directions, distinctions or values? Your answer here may affect your choice of substitute word. And what about *Te*? Here are my suggestions –

Te – virtue, integrity, innocence, power, inner power, moral power, excellence, special, unique, good character.

High Te – organic, self-contained. Virtue or good character that exists for its own sake. Think of the attitude embodied in *Wu-wei* [non-interference]

Low Te – is conscious of the world, which makes it apart from us. Again, using Judeo-Christian imagery, think of Adam and Eve gaining knowledge of good and evil; of feeling shame and separateness from creation.

You may also want to consider the moral attributes of a person travelling their *Tao* – and how these attributes evolve, based on experience and learning. Or consider *Te* as mankind's original unsullied condition, before eviction from the Garden of Eden, if you want to continue with the Judeo-Christian reference.

And a suggestion: since the verse isn't that long, find your favorite translation and type it out, double-spacing with a large, easy-to-read font. Then use search/replace to substitute words. It's important that you read the results aloud, making selection changes until you're comfortable with the sound and meaning you've discovered. Substitute your own words for benevolence, righteousness, propriety and other terms used above. See how these substitutions affect the verse's meaning. Is it possible to have multiple meanings, depending on the translation you use – or the context you're applying it to?

I've adapted this verse from several of my favorite translations. What they share is structure and emphasis, while varying in their wording. The first two comparisons are between high and low *Te*. They're followed by three patterns of behavior and attitude, declining in their adherence to *Tao* and *Te*. And if the listener doesn't get the point in the first section, it's followed by a review showing the consequences of leaving *Tao* and reminding us that we can't tell a book by its cover.

While you can use this interpretation as a starting point, it's important to find a translation that suits your journey. Hopefully you'll find a point on your way where you'll write your own path, one that's different from mine and other interpreters'.

Te, or virtue

Those of highest Te aren't conscious of it. They are virtue. *[They are "in the zone" – in a state of being, rather than a state of consciousness.]*

Those of low Te seek virtue's appearance. They lack true virtue. *[They are conscious of their being or condition.]*

Those of highest Te practice non-action. *[Wu-wei]*

Those of good Te act, even if they don't need to. *[Now we go down a step, from virtue for its own sake to humanity, which entails a self-awareness and identity with others. This has also been called lower virtue or inferior character.]*

Those of lesser Te – or highest morality – act, without any ulterior reason.

Those of highest righteousness act, with a reason or action.

Those of good appearance act, and respond with force when no one responds to them.

Therefore,

When we lose Tao, Te follows.
When we lose Te, humanity follows.
When we lose humanity, imposed rules, regulations and law follow.
When we rely on outside forms, we become stupid.

Therefore those of highest Te recognize substance beneath the skin. They reject appearance and accept substance.

Not happy with your – or my – interpretations for *Te*? Here are some more thought starters that I've seen people use. When you finally find one that you're comfortable with, use it until you grow out of it. Then start again!

- Authenticity
- Character
- Consistency
- Gentleness

- Humanity
- Inner Peace from self-acceptance
- Intrinsic excellence
- Morality
- Personal Power
- Personal Vision
- Reliable
- Righteousness
- Tranquility
- Truth Seeking/Seeker
- Virtuosity
- Virtuousness

The following pages in this chapter discuss *Te* as it's used in the *Tao Te Ching's* different verses. Note that an individual essay may pertain to lines in the middle or the end of a particular verse, or even consecutive verses where a topic is spread between the two. The quote heading one of my commentaries may not be the one at the beginning of a verse, but rather one from its middle, pertaining to our subject.

Practicing *Te*, or virtue – verses and exercises

Verse 10

Can you become like a new-born infant?

Try to remember – the innocence of infancy, where everything and everyone seemed so simple, so good, so easy. Skills were less important than attitude and anything seemed possible.

Try to remember – how a small child's joy can light up a room and bend it to its will.

When you do, you've experienced *Dark Te*. Infants don't distinguish any difference between themselves and the people and objects in their environment. It's only when age institutionalizes them to understand boundaries between themselves and others that they become like the rest of us.

In today's society, many people react to the term "dark" with fear. But when you see it along your *Tao*, consider it hidden and internal, just part of your unconscious metabolism. When your heart [which is usually dark or hidden from most people] walks in *Tao*, your actions can bring joy to others – through example, not commands.

Te, or virtue

This is the basic premise of *Wu-wei,* non-interference: accomplishing all without dominating. Modesty and humility don't cover your light, they are your light. You illuminate others without blinding them.

Be love. Love your life.
Love all around you.
Dark Te is contagious.

If you decide to read through Verse 10 for yourself, you'll most likely find *Dark Te* referred to as hidden, basic, primary, deep, profound, and engraved, among other descriptions. While there may be textual differences there's not a lot of substantive difference.

Should you perform the exercises the verse lists, think about re-writing them to match your age, experience and environment. It'll change the task from academic to practical – one you can hopefully incorporate into your life. You might even want to write or record the exercise to compare with another attempt four or five years from now. Here are some terms you might come across:

元特 – Yuante – dark virtue, internal integrity
元 – Yuan – basic, primary
暗 – An – dark, concealed
隐 – Yin – hidden
深刻 – Shenke – profound
深 – Shen - deep
刻 – Ke – engraved

Verse 21

Your greatest virtue comes only from following the Tao.

No matter how we define our own *Te* – as virtue, integrity, original innocence, or whatever – we still need to practice what we preach. Or, if you want to go into motivational workshop mode, talking the talk isn't enough. Learn to walk the walk.

What's *Te* in your life? Where does it fit into your lifestyle? Please be specific. Describe – maybe even write a few sentences about – a person, place or event in the past week that called on your *Te* in some way.

Happy? Or frustrated with the last exercise? It doesn't really matter. It's more important that you started it, that you planted a seed you can nurture in the coming days and years.

Here's another way of including your own *Te* in everyday life:

Sit back and relax. Think of a beautiful valley – full of magnificent scenery, noble forests, a majestic river, whatever makes it beautiful for you. Now think of raindrops falling on its slopes, of birds dropping twigs, of pebbles and rocks rolling downhill, of giggling children, stalking hunters, grazing deer and prowling mountain lions. They're all converging into this valley, coming over its defining peaks or flowing downstream from a place that's out of your line of vision. The valley's open to them all, without any discrimination. Nature's law will sort things out, maybe letting a bird drop a too-heavy seed-bearing twig that decomposes to fertilize its seed on the forest floor; the human leaving a footstep that allows a puddle to form that breeds a mosquito for a fish to eat, another footprint that kills a seedling, allowing an adjoining plant more room to grow. [And yes, that butterfly flapping its wings to create a hurricane half a world away.] The river continues to flow. Some things will stay, some will go downstream. You'll remember some of this and you'll forget some. But you'll always be receiving new information, new people, new experiences in your life. Like the valley, your body, your self, receives and absorbs everything in your environment, from nasty words and germs to entrancing kisses and refreshing breezes. Some will affect you deeply. Some won't. All without you needing to be conscious of them.

The valley is receptive, open and sometimes even nurturing to new ideas. You don't have to agree with them, but it's nice if you respect others' rights to have them. Oh, and don't forget that those beautiful pearls we get from oysters started out as invasive, irritating bits of grit.

Reading through *Tao* you'll find frequent complimentary references to valleys and channels as the most fertile places in the landscape because they're the lowest, collecting all in their environment. Down is simply a direction, not a negative quality. *Tao* encourages us to be like them – receptive and humble. Be the yin balancing society's yang.

Verse 28

Live the simple life. Be a model all.

This verse encapsulates nearly everything *Tao* says to show us how to build and refine our own *Te*.

And how exactly do we do that?

The answer is frustratingly simple: Follow *Tao*.

OK. Let's get a bit more down to the earth that most of us walk on. Heard about that journey of a thousand steps in verse 64? Here are a few steps to get you started.

First, recognize that not everyone sees the world through your eyes. This doesn't make them bad or wrong, just different. Imagine we're all in the same stadium. Each watching the same game from different seats, on different sides and different levels. Some of us have a great view, others are stuck behind some oversized loudmouths. We're cheering our local team while wearing their colors. Some of us might even be on the field, players giving our all for our side for the length of the match, models for youngsters with dreams of glory. Later, after you've passed through the stadium gates, changed your clothing and rested your voice, you carry on a very civilized relationship with your "opponent." It's sort of like living life in a human body. Once you pass through the pearly gates you discover you have a lot in common with your so-called opponent. You've both been involved in the same sport of life, just from different perspectives.

Keeping in mind that we're all players and fans of some sort, let's try to bring that pre- and post-game civility to our everyday life. And don't forget to think of the tributes paid to individual players by fans of all stripes when they've reached a milestone or undergone some significant life event. Everyone stands, everyone cheers or observes a moment of tribute that extends far beyond local rivalries.

Some people have a vision that you feel complements yours. Others may be uncomfortably opposite. In either case, accept them as the other side of the same coin. Use "the other" not as an enemy, but as an opportunity to learn. Question the reasons others hold other viewpoints. Can you understand where they're coming from? Will this knowledge lead you to teaching or tolerance? Disagreement doesn't need to lead to disrespect.

Oh, and don't forget to question your own beliefs, too. Are they as valid for today's life as they were when you formed them? Or are you at a point in your life where you're looking to make a change – perhaps to change teams or sports?

Don't focus on what you want to eliminate from your life. That gives it power. Replace what's not right for you any more with what fits you now – and is right for your future. Focus on who you are, what you'll do, and who you'll be, all without the part of you you're shedding. You may be familiar with Paul's phrase in *1 Corinthians*, "When I was a child, I spake as a child, I understood as a child, I thought as a child; but when I became a man I put away childish things." Put away what's obsolete for you. But don't throw it away. You might need it again someday. Or someone else, searching through the second-hand shop of ideas, may find your old ones fit them perfectly right now. Be it habits or clothes, what you no longer need may be perfect for another. And remember that not everyone travels the same path as you do. Your brilliant new discoveries may be ideas that others have already used on their journey.

All this is nice for me to say. Why don't you take a break right here to answer these questions using real life situations and people you encounter in your family, job, social circles, and god forbid: religion and politics.

OK, done with your break now? Enjoyed that cup of caffeine or glass of alcohol along with it? Maybe even come to a new understanding of other people or events in your life? Good. And if you haven't, you've just planted some seeds that may sprout in your consciousness in the days and weeks to come.

Here's the next step. It doesn't involve doing anything, just being receptive.

One of *Tao*'s consistent themes encourages people on its path to see themselves as receptors, or receivers, if you will. No matter which translation you use, you'll see repeating references to valleys, watersheds and other physical forms that are open to receive all without judgement. They collect and help along everything without effort and without judgement. Those entering these valleys have their being and perhaps their journeys modified.

But the valley is still the valley, only slightly changed by its visitors. Can you become a valley for others to experience? Just remember not to become a box canyon, blocking others' flow and filling up with garbage.

What happened the last time something new came into your life? Did you react with fear? Or did you respond with curiosity? Can you embrace what's new, the way a river valley absorbs all that flows down its slopes and passing through it, without judgement? Letting each go where they may, recognizing that they're all on their own paths, following their own *Tao*?

Most of us tend to admire people who respect us and are receptive to us, even if they may disagree with us. Can you become a model for others by simply using these two traits: respect and receptivity?

When you have a fullness of life that doesn't require bothering other people, but simply respecting them, a few might follow your example. And a few more might follow theirs. Your way might not be their way and theirs is probably not yours. One size rarely fits all, but most patterns can be adjusted and re-sized to fit others who happen to like that style. And if their style isn't yours, don't wear it.

Some of the steps we've talked about here may be easy for you. Others might require a bit – or a lot – more work. Don't worry. Learning to follow *Tao* is like riding a bicycle: first you have to think, then you have to do, then you're just a bicycle rider – being, not doing.

And when you follow *Tao*, your *Te* increases. At some point along the way your conscious, mechanical contrived doing becomes unconscious *dark Te*. You're no longer a student or a teacher, but a model.

Verse 38

The highest good doesn't come from seeking it, but by becoming it.

And how do we become the good person that people want to be? Well in this case, go back to the chapter's introduction and re-read it. Then do all of its exercises over again, with different examples.

Why?

Because I used this verse as the basis for the chapter introduction just a few pages ago.

Verse 41

Tao hides in invisibility, yet only Tao completes all things.

Next time you're in a car, take a look at the notice on your rear-view mirror: "Objects in mirror are closer than they appear." And, if you've a good memory for movie trivia, you might even recall that rear-mirror view of a dinosaur's tonsils in *Jurassic Park*.

Things – and people – aren't always what they appear to be. How many people recognized that a mild-mannered newspaper reporter was really Superman? Or that the great and powerful Wizard of Oz was really just a down-on-his-luck travelling salesman?

For better or worse, we live in a world that places a premium on style over substance. "Clothes make the man" is a truer axiom than we'd like to believe. Like a child attracted to a shiny toy, many adults are attracted to other age-appropriate [or inappropriate] bling or activities. Take a second now to think of some examples:

- In today's society.
- Among your friends.
- And here's the most important example, yourself.

Don't worry or beat yourself up too much if you're not perfect. None of us are. It's normal. It's the tuition we pay for living in the world. But…is the world your path? Or does your path just happen to run through the world? Whether you're Dorothy sticking to her yellow brick road or an airline pilot on an invisible glide path to a safe landing, we each have our own way, our own *Tao*, for our time here on earth.

A number of religions – those practices that many use as guideposts along their way – proclaim that wealth is a sign that their version of god looks favourably on you. I've found that quite a few people who share this view ignore its complement – that this wealth carries an obligation to help those less fortunate. You can simply look at the *Tao*'s statements on complementarity; or Christ's on the best way to get to heaven in *Luke 18:22* ["Sell all you have and give to the poor."] Remember that many of those who work to accumulate wealth stand out for their avarice as well as for their perceived good. And also remember that you can't take it with you.

Do we own – or simply use – the physical assets that we surround ourselves with? Ownership creates a responsibility for protecting our stuff, caring for it, defending it from those who may want it – all at a great expense. And what, exactly, is your long-term return on investment [ROI] on this great expense?

In the next few pages you'll see examples inspired by some of *Tao*'s examples of *Te*. How many others can you develop?

- In your personal life
- Civic life
- Professional/job life

***Tao's* valleys are empty and receptive**, waiting to be filled. Some translations use the word hollow. Empty buildings, plates and cups are just like *Tao*'s valleys. Their value lies in their availability. Are you empty and prepared to be filled with value? Have you left room in your life for nourishment? Or have you so filled up your life with junk that there's no room for anything of value that might come your way. Sports fans might remember basketball coach Jimmy Valvano, who trained his teams – no matter what their skill level – to always "be in a position to win." One of those overmatched teams won a national championship.

Pervasive *Te* seems deficient. We rarely pay much attention to the immediate environment surrounding us. It's the wallpaper of our lives, always there, always in the background. We rarely notice how it enables us on our path. A river's flood plain seems empty to the ignorant. So they build their cities there and invest more and more financial and emotional capital after every flood. When we realize that the flood plain's emptiness is there for the river's fullness, we plan appropriately, either leaving it alone or restricting our usage to things which will suffer minimum damage when the flood plain fulfills its function.

We all have strengths and weaknesses. In the ideal world we work together in a harmonious balance. In the less-than-ideal world we can at least respect others' abilities and be honest about our own limitations. Many people appear to be deficient only when compared with others' wealth, which is transient. The mass of humanity doesn't have it – and really doesn't need it.

Established *Te* seems weak. Again, we can be blind to our surroundings, just taking for granted the appearance of all that allows our lifestyle. You may have heard the expression about a new broom sweeping clean, but the old broom knows the corners best. Established *Te* is an old broom. Like many of us, it's been young once, with all the strength and vigor of youth. Now, like the bamboo and willows, it has roots that let it survive the winds that topple others who make a show of appearing strong.

Verse 49

The good I declare good. The bad I also declare good.

We're all creatures sharing this earth. And it's human nature to act in our own self-interest. But it's how we define ourselves that drives this behavior. Does our self-interest end with our body, that individual hunk of flesh, bone and brain that's out for its own comfort and preservation? Or does it extend to a larger self, be it a family, a team, a tribe or a species? Or perhaps to the exterior system that supports it?

People can be tall or short, skinny or fat, near-sighted or far-sighted. We all have our strengths and weaknesses, experience and ignorance. We don't expect the exploring infant to know why it should keep its fingers from the fan. Or the stranger from distant lands to know our customs. Do we curse and punish people for their ignorance – or create teaching moments? Do we teach with a talk or a stick? Lead by example or a loud voice? Show and tell or coerce and punish?

Are people bad – or do they just have different priorities and codes? Do you know their point-of-view? Many times it's more than just nice-to-know. It's need-to-know.

Keep your own integrity – and let them keep theirs.

How would you like to be treated? When you're in a position where you're unsure, or about to make a significant error, or in a situation where you're way over your head?

Oh, and don't forget that "idiot" on the road in front of you. Are they creeping along below the speed limit because they see something ahead that you're blind to? Or are they speeding to get their passenger to the hospital? When you don't know the reason for someone's actions, think about cutting them some slack. And, even if you're fully aware of why a person is doing something you don't care for, why get excited when it's beyond your control. Just use them as a teaching moment, for yourself or for others.

Don't agree with me? How about a teacher who wandered through the Middle East a couple of thousand years ago? You can read some of his comments on how to deal with enemies in *Mathew 5:43-48* or *Luke 6:27-36*. Abraham Lincoln reminded us to treat others with "malice toward none and charity for all." [2nd Inaugural Address]. More recently, you might want to take a look at the aftermath of World Wars I and II. The punitive Versailles Treaty of 1919 laid the groundwork for World War II. The 1948 Marshall Plan aimed at recovery and laid the groundwork for restoring the European economy.

In a world where you can be anything, be kind
>   -Attributed to the 14th Dalai Lama

Verse 51

The Tao births and nurses all. But does not own them.

Believe in the essential goodness of people? Then you probably let them do what comes naturally without fearing disaster. If this isn't our belief system and we create rules to control people, those who don't need rules will follow them and many who don't like them will ignore or break them. The golden mean that people, organizations and governments aspire to is to make things easy and efficient for honest people and difficult for hardened criminals and fraudsters.

When we look at *Tao* as a direction with guideposts rather than a paved highway with signposts, we trust people to find their personal path. *Tao* is the good *Te*-filled parent, providing sustenance while giving freedom. And what makes that good parent we should emulate? One whose virtue – their *Te* – is just a natural part of their personality? OK, for most of us this is the ideal, not the real. We express our love in different ways and, because we're human, occasionally make decisions that we later realize may not have been optimal. Note that while I'm using the term parent, these notes could just as easily apply to anyone in an authority position, be they a leader, supervisor, mentor or holding some similar role. As the oft-ignored business axiom goes, "Get good people. Then get out of their way."

In the ideal world, the best parent practices *Wu-wei*, giving their child room to grow while making sure that it's a safe, not claustrophobically sheltering and smothering, environment. In this context, it's called *Dark Te* or hidden virtue, because it's just part of their nature. It's who they are.

Look at a child learning to walk or to ride a bike. At first, the good parent is there to help and guide. But if a parent never lets the child walk or ride on their own, their muscles and balance will never develop. The over-active parent creates a weak and dependent child. This doesn't mean that we ignore the child [or employee or anyone else in our temporary charge], it simply means that we allow them freedom to grow, which usually means making a mistake or three.

The Taoist, full of *Te*, knows the balance between neglect and smothering. It's the Goldilocks approach, not too much of one or the other, but just the right amount at the right times. *Tao* calls it *Wu-wei* or non-interference. Plant a seed and nourish it. But if it's to grow & bear fruit, it needs to learn how to survive in the elements. [Did you know that the best wines come from poor soils, where the plant needs to work to grow?]

Our charges, be they children, employees or others subject to our position in life, need to learn life by themselves, through experience, not talk. Would Dorothy have ever discovered that there's no place like home if she hadn't followed the yellow brick road? And if you're not familiar with Rumpsringa, the Amish tradition of teenagers leaving their community to experience the outside world, now might be a good time to leave this page and spend a few minutes searching the web. The vast majority of these teens, after experiencing the outside world, return to their family roots and traditions.

Te, or virtue

So what's a loving parent to do?

Consider the lesson of the Prodigal Son [*Luke 15:11-32*]. The young man's father never stopped loving him and welcomed him home with loving arms and generosity. Jesus compared the father to his heavenly father, in contrast to the vengeful brother, who represented the hidebound Pharisees of the day.

Not into Christian imagery? You may want to study Mahayana Buddhism. While there are obvious cultural differences and approaches between Chapter 4 of the Lotus Sutra and the Gospel of Luke, the core message is the same, the loving father welcomed his son home.

Not into religion at all? An Italian named Carlo Collodi published a book in 1883 containing characters you may have heard of – Pinocchio and his father, Geppetto. While Disney changed some details, the core message remains the same.

Remember that this is one of *Tao's* many verses that contrast ritual-encrusted Confucianism with *Tao's* organic, shamanic roots. No matter where your personal *Tao* takes you, you might want to consider this verse from both perspectives: law-and-order and laissez-faire. Can you open your mind to appreciate another side's point-of-view? Is there such a thing as a middle-of-the-road approach that incorporates the best of both worlds? Can you see yourself occupying these different roles at different times of your life: prodigal Pinocchio, his loving father, and the bible's rules-and-regulations brother?

Verse 54

Abundance and growth come from firm foundations.

Sometimes we don't need an interpreter. This is one of those verses that stands on its own, no matter which term you use to define *Te*.

If you want to generate more virtue, start with yourself. Then move out in your life: to your family, community, country and the world, until you've encompassed everyone and everything. Sort of like planting a small seed that grows to feed many. Or the pebble in the pond that generates rings that reach to shore.

How do we do this? By observing – and then using what we learn to become an example for others. Sounds simple. But in today's world of complexity and clutter, can we follow the KISS formula [Keep it simple, s…]? The answer, of course, is yes. Start with yourself, in the now. Deal with larger organisms later. What should you start with? That's your call, but you can most likely follow the example of someone or something you admire.

Be patient. The world isn't waiting for you to save it. Most likely, neither is your country or your community. But if you can make changes in your life that affect your attitude, your health or your being for the better, they may affect your family.

So…pick one practice that you want to add or subtract from your life. Take a look at how others – people you admire – are handling it. Then day-by-day, week-by-week for however long it takes make this change part of your metabolism.

When that's done, start with another.

OK, now it's time to stop reading and talk to yourself. Remember that definition of *Te* you found that you liked in the introduction to this section? How can you increase it in your personal life? Try not to focus on what to eliminate, since that only gives it strength. Focus on what will replace what you're leaving behind. Fill your life with so much good that there's no room for what doesn't work for you.

Te, or virtue

Verse 55

He who is filled with Te has a child's purity.

Verse 55 builds on verse 54, giving us a starting point for self-transformation – or is it really self-regeneration?

If you're going to find or build your personal *Te*, it's best to start with your true self – not the institutionalized, scar-strengthened, armor-plated shell that most of us have grown to protect ourselves in today's world – but with the primal innocence we lost along the way.

As you read through this verse it's easy to see reasons for building our armor – it's filled with lots of creatures willing to do us harm. But when you study it a bit more deeply you may see it as returning to *Tao's* shamanic roots, into a Garden of Eden where all creatures lived together in harmony.

If we can find our way back to the Garden, we can discover some of that open-mindedness we may have abandoned. There's so much in nature that we ignore because we focus just on our own kind. So much in other people we're blind to because we focus on ourselves. Most of us live in a society that values ego-driven activity. To return to Eden's harmony we need to recall – and use – the principle of *Wu-wei*.

What are the toxic parts of your life – the stinging insects, wild beasts and birds of prey we find in the verse? How do you neutralize them? Can you fill your life with so many "good" things that there's no room for the undesirables? Can you find a way to eliminate these toxic people and things from your environment? You know the verse and the process: Make a list of the naughty and nice. Check it twice. Then act on it. Create step-by-step plans, with the baby steps first. After all, if you're looking to change your life, it's nice to have some early successes for encouragement.

Changing the natural is against the *Tao*. Isn't our objective to return to living in the *Tao*, full of *Te*?

Verse 59

Teaching people or serving heaven, there is nothing better than moderation.

Once upon a time...

There was a troublesome little girl named Goldilocks who broke into a house owned by some bears. She ate their porridge and broke their chairs before going upstairs to mess up their beds. We can give the bears credit for exercising moderation by allowing her to escape and not eating her in place of their porridge before using her bones to repair the chair.

And what do we remember most about her? That she tested and tried things until she found the one that was just right – not too hot or cold, not too big or small, not too hard of soft.

For our purposes today, we'll focus on just one of the morals of the story: the value of moderation.

When was the last time you had a bowl of soup that started out w-a-a-y too hot? And then, after you let it cool, you found that it was really too cold to taste good. Have you ever looked forward to that bowl of ice cream or ice-cold drink on a hot day, only to get hit with brain freeze?

Not into food comparisons? Then think of work. Or play. Or anything else that we know can be carried to extremes [like driving too fast – or too slowly – on a motorway.]

And don't forget that all work and no play make Jack/Jane pretty dull. The best employers know that rested and refreshed employees do better work. The best coaches recognize the enthusiasm and joy that comes from students released from their word-and-paper-filled classrooms.

Balancing life is sometimes difficult, with rest occasionally enforced by illness or accident. I found by happenstance that I was able to balance my professional paper-pushing and travel with the physical work of carpentry and the other tasks involved with rehabbing old homes. But when the physical release evolved into work without play, I found that travel and learning for me – and not for my clients – gave me the balance my brain needed.

Balance helps you stay on your *Tao*. As a ruler, a mentor, an example to others, you can become the deep roots, the balancing or reference point for others. There's no need to tell others how to live, but if you maintain moderation in your own life, they'll see the benefits.

Show others, don't tell them.

Verse 60

Ruling a big country is like frying small fish. Too much poking spoils the meal.

Verse 60 continues Verse 59's advice, talking about balance. If you have just the right touch you won't over-do things. And what's the right touch? Living in accordance with *Wu-wei*. You pay attention to conditions and let environment do the work. The cook isn't responsible for the fish, but for the flame and pan that will actually do the cooking, along with adding whatever spices will flavor the fish. When they've done their job all the cook needs to do is to remove the ready-to-eat fish that the heat and assorted spices have prepared.

"Too much poking" is also a sideswipe at the rules-and-regulations Confucianism of that day – and this day – as well. Many times people are oblivious to practices until they're forbidden. Then curiosity arises. You may be familiar with the Carl Sandburg verse adapted for the long-running play, *The Fantasticks*: "Why did the kids pour jam on the cat...put beans in their ears? ... They did it because we said no."

If you don't forbid something, many people will never even be aware of it. [Until now, have you ever considered pouring jam on a cat or putting beans in your ears?]

Verse 68

Non-competition is harmony… and power.

In a verse that talks of generals, warriors and leaders, is there a message for the rest of us? Think for a moment. How do you calm a crying child – with shouts and threats, or calm diversion? Whether it's children under your authority or work and social equals, you'll find that the ancient aphorism usually works pretty well: "You can catch more flies [or anything else] with honey than vinegar."

I know and agree that sometimes you just have to put out the fire. But once you've gained short-term peace, what's the easiest way to prevent future fires? Do you work with others by creating fear of punishment or seeding enthusiastic compliance? If you want to spend your entire life dealing with problems, maybe the punishment option could work. But as soon as [a] you take a break or [b] others figure out ways around you, you've failed.

If you've found that physical force or verbal violence gets results, ask yourself if it's the result you really need. You might affect others' behavior, but have you really changed their motivation? An apple's flesh can be bruised and beaten, but it protects the core. The core is the future. No matter how much you bite or bruise an apple, its flesh still protects its seeds. In fact, when you bruise it, you begin breaking down the flesh, so it becomes fertilizer for the seeds of more apples more quickly. In the words of Irish patriot Terence MacSwiney, "It is not those who inflict the most but those who suffer the most who prevail."

Want to kick back, relax and perhaps move on to something else? Plant seeds with education and encouragement. Plant them in yourself before even thinking of planting them in others. Be their model, not their nagging taskmaster.

Throughout Tao you'll see references to *Dark Te*. This is a *Te* that's more than just your behavior, It's part of your core metabolism. It doesn't really matter whether you're using yoga, meditation, or something else – there are hundreds of disciplines – one or a blend of several will be right for you. Work from the inside out, not the outside in.

Verse 79

The Tao doesn't take sides.

Ever disagree with someone? And still disagreed with them even after the two of you have made what passes for peace?

Inertia is one of the basic laws of physics – and it applies to humans as well as other creatures and objects. While we'd love to say that it's knowledge, experience, devotion and other virtues that keep us on our paths, in many cases it's just inertia. And don't forget that your path may be different from another's. [If two people agree on something, is one of them redundant?]

OK, that's the easy part. Recognize that behavior may not always reflect attitude. We can affect one, but not the other. Deal with it.

But what about that voice inside your head? Are your heart and mind one – or are you always wanting to be somewhere else doing something else with somebody else? Any place but here and now. Are you trying to go two places and be two different people at the same time? Sounds exhausting. And it is. You don't wear clothes in the shower. Or a winter coat in the summer. Or sandals in the winter. So why wear all these superfluous clothes/thoughts in your head wherever you go?

So what's a Taoist to do?

Follow your own *Tao*, building your *Te* using the principles of *Wu-wei*. Yes, that's easier said than done. And if you're concerned about three Chinese words in the same sentence it might mean that you've come upon this section at random. Not a problem, since there's no need to read *Tao Te Ching* or many other works in sequence.

In the context of this particular verse, simply remember to be true to your core values – and to respect others in theirs. We don't have to agree with others to get along with them.

Find a way to focus, let the non-essentials fall away. It may mean sitting down and making a formal list of priorities. Then you can set deadlines and tactics for sanely replacing those practices and people that don't suit you anymore. Let your "essentials" fill the time and mental attention you used to devote to what you've left behind.

Then, when you've completed your list, start the process over again.

Your goal?

Just be.

Oh, and one more thing, since friends reading this verse asked if Abraham Lincoln was a Taoist because he's reputed to have said "My concern is not whether the Lord is on our side; my greatest concern is to be on God's side."

Of course I can't answer the question. But I can point out that Lincoln, like many other people and sources [including the *Tao Te Ching*], have statements attributed to them that they never said.

One version of this pronouncement was attributed to him by a clergyman in a funeral eulogy. Another version, with different wording and context, appeared in a book written by Lincoln's portrait painter a year after Lincoln's death. There's no record of Lincoln saying it in public.

So, did he really say it? Does it really matter?

What's more important? The messenger? The message? Or the practice that the message brings?

Wu-Wei – an introduction

Wu-Wei is one of the most commonly misunderstood aspects of *Tao*. Its glyphs are usually translated as inaction or non-action. Better interpretations would be non-intrusive action or non-wasted action. The point is to stay in sync with your environment so you don't interfere with natural processes. Then, when conditions are right, you work with them and they work with you and for you, instead of against you. Life's a whole lot easier when our actions are in harmony with our surroundings and you don't have to contrive things.

If you're looking for a good restaurant dinner, you don't arrive in the morning when only the clean-up crew is around. You wait until the kitchen and dining room are fully staffed and ready to serve you. Skilled jujitsu practitioners let their attackers commit to a course then, with minimal action and maximum skill, win the match by using their opponent's strength against them. It's all in the timing, in knowing when, where and how much action is appropriate for any situation. Years ago a flight instructor instilled in me the principle that a wise pilot uses their superior knowledge and skills to avoid needing to use their superior knowledge and skills. Read the winds of your life and you'll be a better pilot, sailor or person.

Many of us have been to recitals and performances by beginners, who are mechanically correct in everything they do, but leave us cringing because they lack the flow of easy understanding, of being one with their subject. Their music, their dance, their sport, their whatever, is what they do, not who they are. Think of learning to ride a bike, play a piano, or juggle objects. In the beginning, we're using our mind to learn. At a certain point we leave our mind behind and learn by feel, because the mind interferes with our flow of doing. We ride and perform our task instinctively, never using the conscious part of our brain. When we reach this point, we're "going with the flow" or "in the zone" as we've heard many athletes and musicians describe how their best performances are characterized by a relaxed focus or single-mindedness on the task at hand. They're not performing, they've become the performance. An environment's non-essentials simply fall from their consciousness into the wallpaper. Is a joyous child splashing in a puddle thinking or simply being at one with their world?

Wu-Wei, or non-action

Non-action doesn't mean becoming a hermit and dropping out of society. Nor does it mean surrendering to structured rituals which may not be appropriate for a particular occasion.

Instead, it suggests that we recognize our situation and work with it. Most times we'll find that it's usually easier to use our energy to take steps that allow others to do their work. Why force something that's not ready when, with much less effort, we can create conditions that allow nature to take its course. Plant a seed now. Later on its fruits will nourish you. [Or, from the plant's perspective, it lets you plant and nurture it so that it can reproduce.]

Recognize that there's a harmony in the universe. The stars shine, the planets move and the rest of creation can do very well without human intervention. Remember that we're simply part of the universe, not its controller. When you enter this lifetime, please check your ego at the door.

> *There is a tide in the affairs of men, which taken at the flood, leads to fortune. Omitted, all the voyage of their life is bound in shallows and miseries...We must take the current when it serves, or lose our ventures.*
>
> Brutus
Julius Caesar
Act IV, Sc 3

This chapter discusses *Wu-Wei* as it's used in the *Tao Te Ching's* different verses. Note that an individual essay may pertain to lines in the middle or the end of a particular verse, or even consecutive verses where a topic is spread between the two. The quote heading one of my commentaries may not be the one at the beginning of a verse, but rather one from its middle, pertaining to our subject.

Practicing *Wu-Wei*, or non-action – verses and exercises

Verse 2

The wise ruler manages with non-action

But if you're devoted to non-action, how do you get things done?

That's a fair question, but only if you're grounded in the "action" part of life's equation, where we feel the need to create, organize or do something. While this may satisfy our ego, it may or may not be appropriate for the bigger picture we all live in. When we look at life and the universe in their entirety this seeming contradiction assumes clarity. Simply put, non-action is just the other side of a coin. To be more respectful to the original meaning of the Chinese characters, we may want to begin thinking "spontaneous" and "contrived" instead of "non-action" and "action." How can we define "action" if we don't have something to compare it to? This contrast is essentially what we see in this verse's comparisons: hard/easy, long/short, high/low and so on.

Rather than look at these examples as opposites, consider seeing them as end points on a continuum. When you listen to your inner Sage – or conscience if you prefer – you'll act, but in a reasoned, efficient manner. Sometimes you'll just act spontaneously, from your heart. In either case there's no need to exhaust yourself creating conditions for success if you're in a place where those conditions are already assembling themselves from other sources [or if you're in another place, where they'll *never* come together]. Wait until the time is right, then take action. You'll achieve your goal with the most efficient energy use.

It's said that the ancient Egyptians had two different verbs for procrastination. One carried much the same meaning that we use today, a negative description of laziness. The other was in the spirit of *Tao*: Use your intelligence to avoid unnecessary tasks. One of these practices is through another of *Tao*'s continuing themes, humility. If you don't attach your ego or your name to a task, you'll find that many more people will buy into it. You'll achieve the same result with a lot less work. And if the end result isn't what you anticipated? No need to worry. Since you never laid claim to it, you haven't lost anything.

In *Tao*, non-action doesn't mean no action. It means no wasted action.

Do what's necessary. Don't contrive things to keep busy or to make yourself look good. Oh, and don't forget to check your ego at the door.

Verse 3

Practice non-doing. Everything falls into place.

The good leader – of a nation, a business or a family – recognizes that it's easier to create conditions to encourage people's behavior than it is to micro-manage their lives. Make it easy for people to do what's best. When you restrict what people are able to see, have, or do, you're creating temptation, that natural tendency nearly everyone shares: to want what we can't have. Remember that the best of our underlings will be smart enough [and the worst will be ignorant enough] to find loopholes and exploit the rules and regulations to create those infamous unintended consequences.

It's one thing to "teach your children", but if you do this through formal classwork, structured job descriptions or legal requirements you're creating an environment of opposites that in its own way encourages people to actively search outside the box you'd like to keep them in. As children, how many of us preferred the daydreams arising from the window-view of that wide world outside to the droning of our classroom's teacher? Change the venue to a meeting room or a church today. Has our attitude changed? Or just our ability to split our awareness and maintain the appearance of attention?

With us or without us, people will still want to go their own way. But if we can create an environment around ourselves that's desirable, it will attract them. And if you create a really good environment, they'll be attracted to it, not you. In the business world, I remember that our best clients weren't the ones we chased and pitched, but the ones who came to us because they'd seen the work we did for others or were referred to us by existing clients. When I was looking for tenants for the old houses I'd fixed up, the best ones were always referrals from current or former tenants. [They were former tenants because, after a number of years with me, they'd saved enough money to buy a house. Then they'd call me for referrals on plumbers and other tradesmen they needed for their own property.]

What do we need to do to become the goal – or the source – of people's aspirations, rather than the trigger for their escapist daydreams?

Verse 8

Those above reproach are those who don't contend.

Years ago I worked for a man who made a point of telling us to take "well days" as well as sick days. When those first beautiful days of spring arrive, when we needed to take time to prepare for some special family occasion, or for any similar reason, he knew that our mental refreshment was more important to the quality of work we did than our physical presence in the workplace. His only requirement – a reasonable one – was that we all didn't desert the building on the same day. While this practice may not be appropriate for every person in every workplace, the attitude could be.

You may recall the story of Canute, king of England and most of Scandinavia a bit more than a thousand years ago. Growing exhausted from his fawning aides' continuous and obsequious praise, he went down to the ocean and commanded the waves to stop. We know the result. [At least with the waves. Hopefully he imbued his court with a dose of reality, as well.] So… rather than fighting the currents of life – or building your house on sand – learn to surf through life. And to avoid too much sun. Or you may want to emulate the ancient Egyptians, who used the Nile's floods as the basis of their agriculture. Or you can always waste your life climbing uphill on that sand dune that's quickly washed away in next season's flood.

You may want to take a look at life from this perspective –

Think for a moment – better yet, feel, for several moments, that energy we have after a truly restful sleep, opening our eyes to a beautiful day. Or of that quiet, unspoken peace radiating from a sleeping child, a comforting fireplace or a task well-done.

How can we replicate this peace throughout our lives?

Most likely not by planning and organizing – unless your planning and organizing is designed to create a conducive environment. Otherwise you're treating yourself the same way the parent treats the child when they order them to, "Sit down, shut up and tell me everything you did today."

Don't put your life in a straightjacket when you can curl your toes in the sand.

Verse 11

Emptiness is available for use. Fullness isn't.

How many times have you heard the motivational speaker-du jour expound on "potential"? It's usually something that's out there, not here with you. And how do you fulfill it? By following their steps, which usually requires investing more time and even more money with them.

The *Tao* talks of potential, as well. It's our core, the inner self that's invisible to most others. Admire the next beautiful building you happen to see. Where does its potential lie? In that magnificent façade – or the functional design of its mechanicals and interior floorplan? What about that massive warehouse or truck depot out near the airport or railroad? Do those weathered walls and that patched roof impair its function as a storage and transit point? Does your favorite stained and chipped coffee mug perform any differently than a sparkling new one straight from the shop?

It's fine to admire a structure, be it a tree's shape, a canyon's curves and layers, or any other object constructed by man or nature. But remember the maxim coined by architect Louis Sullivan, "Form follows function." Whatever we create – in ourselves or for others – should be suitable for the function it will contain. We build to assist, not to obstruct. To contain for use, not to hoard.

Your action, if you're living in *Tao*? It's creating conditions – building the visible or invisible structure that allows life to grow in an organic, natural manner.

Your non-action? It's up to you.

How can you "let go" to give yourself to the emptiness, to the potential, within you?

Verse 15

Avoid being over-full. Be ready for life.

Feeling stuffed after that big meal? Have you ever loaded yourself or your vehicle with so much that it's difficult to start moving and nearly impossible to maneuver? Then how can you truly appreciate a delicious dessert? Or take advantage of a wonderful opportunity that suddenly appears in your face?

But we can't starve ourselves or waste cargo space. And the answer is not to simply repeat what you or someone else has done before – because it's now, not then. Conditions have probably changed.

The answer, to nobody's surprise, is balance. When we balance our lives – work and play, nourishment and exercise – we're reflecting *Tao*'s complementarity. Just as we're members of a society of humans and a civilization of planets, our body is a society of cells and organs. Each requires periods of action and non-action to be at their best.

So…use your brain – and your heart – to figure out what's best for you. Then take a break. And don't forget to give your mind a rest, too. And that's when those little brain bubbles will start popping in, just like you see in cartoons. Most of our days fill our minds with a confusing collection of to-do lists, media input, daily responsibilities and everything else that assaults our peace and quiet. When we let all the clutter of today's daily life and planning for futures that may or may not happen just settle to the bottom of our consciousness, we'll find some clear space that may be open to occupation by thoughts, views and feelings we might not have considered before.

Who knows? You might like these new ideas. Or they may reinforce your earlier decisions. Either way, that rest period – full of non-action – works for you. Remember, all work and no play make…

Verse 30

Force leads to troubles. Tao to peace.

Remember those magic words we were taught to use when we were children?

"Please." And, "Thank you."

Most of us have found that their regular use opens many doors for us. People are usually more inclined to be generous to polite people than to the pushy. And once those doors are open, our access to their contents may well be greater than that given to rude people who just push their way in. Some people might call this the law of karma – if you live by the sword, you'll die by it. Personally, I like the easier way. The return on our investment in kindness [or spoonfuls of sugar] is far greater than any investment in force. It's usually easier to disarm people by killing them with kindness than by killing them with weapons. It doesn't matter if the weapon is a warlike military, an advertising-driven marketing plan or new tactics on a sporting field. Those using weapons need to keep using weapons because those they use them against will come back with more, most likely more powerful, ones.

And who benefits, besides the weapons-makers?

Verse 34

You can achieve great things when you don't seek greatness.

Look at *Tao* as the [hopefully] benevolent parents who birthed us. Children feel that they're running free, rarely realizing the support and protection surrounding them. Or be like the mature river, gently carrying all as it flows to the sea. Be they fish, boats, people or branches, they're all treated equally and all are carried to their destination. Even if they're not aware of it, this same river nourishes the plants that feed the fish and people and provide wood for their boats.

Living in *Tao* doesn't mean that we don't interfere to help or protect someone. It means we ensure that conditions are favorable for them, so that we most likely won't have to interfere. Others are oblivious to our presence and we're free of their demands.

Verse 37

No desire, yet nothing is left undone.

When you need nothing more than what you already have, do you still want more? Why?

Why not wait for that breeze to bring you refreshment, for time to bring you that holiday joy, for those you love to achieve their goals. There's nothing you can do to make the clock's hands or the globe turn faster, so relax.

When we want what we don't have, or what we can't have now [or ever], all we're doing is churning up our stomach acid and wasting physical, emotional and mental energy that could be better spent appreciating what we already have and who we already are.

Serenity – the feeling of satisfaction and joy that comes from just being. Whether it's appreciating another's joy, the fullness of a good meal or the crackling warmth of a fireplace, it's when we're not analyzing the present, looking forward to our next task or backward to what we did or didn't do. Is it possible to keep this feeling, this peace, this attitude, in every moment of every day?

And what do we call this desire for a state of non-desire?

Wu-Wei, or non-action

Verse 38

The highest good doesn't come from seeking it, but by becoming it.

We've all seen – and usually admired – people with a natural talent for something, be it sports, business, or some other field. They don't need to think about what they do because it just flows naturally from them. In the "best" cases their doing is their being, their oneness. The rest of us, with varying degrees of aptitude, skill and a lot of hard work, can sometimes approach the star's level of expertise, but rarely their comfort with it.

And you may have heard the anecdote about the best way to destroy a tennis pro's serve: it's simply to ask him or her a question about its mechanics – do they breathe before or after they toss the ball, how many fingers and where do they place them on the ball, and so forth. You're taking their natural flow, their being, and converting it to a mechanical process. This is the reason why natural athletes are rarely good coaches. They're unaware of the step-by-step process the rest of us need to approach a level of competency that's still far below their level. Apply this same analogy to music, dance or any other field where the subject's natural aptitude comes from their brain synapses connecting at a rate that's far beyond what the rest of us can imagine. [Of course, there are probably things we can do in the same manner that are baffling to them.]

When we're "in the flow" we're being, not acting. This spontaneity is the core of what *Tao* calls *Wu-wei*. While it's sometimes translated as non-action, its true meaning is non-fabrication – the avoidance of artificiality. It's only those who haven't yet developed their particular talent who need to act in a step-by-step manner.

And by the way…if you're one of those experts, or on a learning path to become one, remember not to lord it over those who may not have your skills. There's no reason to make others feel inferior, particularly because there are undoubtedly some things they do and know that will dwarf your skill and knowledge. Have you ever noticed that the most sanctimonious, holier-than-thou, better-than-you people are trying way too hard to overcome some sort of insecurity?

Be glad you're learning, be glad you're skilled. Share gracefully, without putting on airs.

Verse 41

Tao is hidden and nameless. This is how things get done.

Sometimes we just don't get it. No matter how hard – and how many different ways – someone tries to explain something to us, it's just beyond our comprehension. And other times the shoe's on the other foot, where we realize that we're wasting our time on an issue that's beyond another's comprehension.

It could be a case of casting pearls before swine – or as it's sometimes told: "Never try teaching a pig to sing. It wastes your time and annoys the pig." [*Matthew 7:6* and Mark Twain, among others]

Or maybe you haven't prepared your student properly. It's hard teaching quantum physics to someone who hasn't yet learned to add and subtract.

So what are we to do?

As with many other questions, the answer is, "It depends." If another's ignorance is not harming themselves or the greater good, why waste your energy and their time? If, on the other hand, you see a potential for harm [or greater good], appropriate action – followed by a lesson that doesn't sound like a lesson – may be appropriate.

The *Tao*, among many paths, talks of problems that arise when ignorance reigns. Today we even have scientific studies to document the old axiom that fools rush in where angels fear to tread. The more a person knows, the more they realize that there's a lot they don't know. Ignorant people don't know what they don't know and can assume they "know it all." If you'd like to learn more about this phenomenon, research on the Dunning-Kruger Effect will probably answer most of your questions. Hopefully it won't make you overly cynical.

Verse 43

Few comprehend teaching without words or understand the value of non-action.

Feel better now? Very few people are perfect. But that doesn't mean we can't try. But trying is the way to imperfection, not perfection! Consider just being, not consciously teaching others, but living a life they may want to emulate, but only if their path happens to resemble ours. Showing them without showing off. Respecting, living with and benefiting from our environment.

Look at it this way: We all need water. But does water need us? So we welcome water by providing spaces for it to collect. When we allow this environment for water to "just be" we benefit from all that water is. Water naturally seeks its own level and in the long run there's not a lot we can do about it. Sounds a lot like people, doesn't it?

Non-action is another way of saying that we accept this principle – that people, nature and things will always return to their true nature, no matter what we say or do. Think of all the times rivers have flooded over our carefully engineered banks and levees. Of course, there are times when we need to deal with symptoms – natural flooding and human temper tantrums – in the short term. But the Taoist recognizes their role in the natural scheme of things and adjusts accordingly: dealing with the short term and planting seeds for the long term. Many times we'll find that haste really does make waste. Don't rush in to solve today's problem. It may evaporate on its own before this time next week.

Tired of all the water imagery in *Tao*? Then consider electricity. It doesn't do anything. But its presence allows light bulbs and other appliances to operate. The light bulb is a tool that allows electricity to help us. Without power it's an inert object. But just as water can flood those in the lowlands, lightning can strike those standing up on hilltops. Teach by being, not by standing out.

Why do people work so hard to stop what's naturally going to happen anyway, when it might be easier to live with it and enjoy it? Living with nature is a lot easier than imposing ourselves on it.

Verse 47

The Sage sees clearly without looking,
accomplishes much without doing.

The child focuses on their toy and the moment – while the parent sees their past and future. The salesman works to convince a customer to buy an item, while his marketing director knows how this item fits not only into the customer's business and his own manufacturing process, but how the world is changing and what will replace this item. The homemaker looks beyond the meal they're serving, knowing what will be available for future meals.

These are holistic views, looking at the bigger picture while not ignoring what's in front of us. You may want to contrast this approach with the western scientific approach, which breaks everything down to its components – the expert being one who knows more and more about less and less until they know everything about nothing. Others will contrast it with task-driven business and political environments, with "management by objective." There's nothing wrong with any of these, as long as we also maintain a focus on the bigger picture. Without this perspective, it's easy to become the king who killed the goose laying golden eggs.

Verse 48

Seeking Tao? Lose something every day.

You may recognize a more recent version of this aphorism, told in *Luke 18:22*, where Jesus told the rich man, "Sell all you have and give to the poor…come, follow me."

The first part of this admonition might be somewhat difficult for those tied to all their things, but it makes sense in the long run. [Remember, you can't take it with you.] Do you really want to be like the medieval nobility who donated their castles and vineyards to the monasteries just to guarantee themselves better treatment in the afterlife? Or the ones who contributed to cathedral-building in exchange for their highly visible stadium box – excuse me, personal chapel – nearest the altar and their face reproduced as the face of an archangel or saint when a famous painter created a portrait of heaven?

If we're looking for return-on-investment in charity, is it really charity? Act from your heart, not your ego. Believe it or not, what others think of you really isn't that important.

Maybe a change of perspective might be helpful. We're part of the planet, in whatever sub-order you care to identify with – family, tribe, genus, species, whatever lifeform works for you. The important thing is to be a team player. Even if you're not a sports fan, you're probably aware that most teams keep statistics on assists, because they lead to point-scoring. Office environments have essential staff that allow the names on the door to do what they do best. Without these unsung heroes the big-name heroes wouldn't be half as effective at what they do. When we recognize our own strengths and weaknesses and work with Mother Nature as a participant, not an overlord, we all win.

Leave space in your life for things that last – if it's something you didn't have before, it's probably something you can live without.

Oh, and one more thing, don't forget to accept people for who they are, not what they have.

Verse 57

Win the world with non-action.

Nobody has your vision. And none of us really knows what's going on in the minds of others. One person's tool can easily become another's weapon. The Wright Brothers invented a flying machine. The military made it into fighters and bombers. Social media pioneers created ways for people to communicate, to see their businesses subverted by trolls and propagandists. If you recall the lesson of *Jurassic Park*, just because we can do something, should we?

Is the world we live in a Pandora's Box – or a holiday present from a favorite relative? Accept that there will be well-meaning people who accidently do wrong. And that some of the ill-intentioned will accidently do good.

What's your role in life? Does everyone else have to do things your way? Perhaps they know more about their specialties than you do. And even if they're ignorant of the way you think things should be done, consider the case of George Boole. He's the 19th Century mathematician who invented Boolean algebra, the basis for much of today's computer technology. He never had formal mathematical training and was ignorant of his era's mathematical conventions. So without these blinders he proceeded to solve problems in what he saw as the best manner, creating a new and better way of doing things.

Ignorance can create that fresh set of eyeballs that so many of us need when we're in the middle of something, whether it's proofreading or working on something that you've been doing the same way forever from inertia, ignoring the fact that the environment has changed and your project may have become off-target at best and obsolete at worst.

Just because your predecessors did something one way doesn't mean you have to. Hopefully they did what was appropriate for their times. Hopefully, you'll do what's appropriate for your times.

Verse 58

The Sage shines without blinding.

Verse 58 is simply an extension of the previous one. How many times have you heard the phrases "hidden blessings" and "unintended consequences"? Whether you're a family, a business or a government, if you plan every detail, you're depriving people of opportunities to grow and use their creativity. Then when the surprise occurs, as it always will, your people are unprepared to deal with it and you're worse off than before.

Consider that it'll probably be easier for you – and more satisfying for those relying on you – if you're a guiding light instead of a tour guide. Let people approach your being at their own pace, not yours. And you know something? Their path may not be your path, but your light will illumine their way, anyway.

Verse 63

Act with non-action.

Through the years most of us have encountered people who'll promise anything to make you feel good in the moment, but never follow through. Used car salesmen and quite a few home improvement contractors come to mind. Like the little boy crying "wolf!" they eventually lose their credibility. One of the reasons I picked up homebuilding skills was that I didn't trust the tradesmen I could afford and couldn't afford the ones I respected.

Then there are the people who build magnificent structures – buildings, businesses, ideas – without placing them on firm foundations. No matter how impressive the structure, it's bound to fail. Think of that bell tower in Pisa, Italy. Do you really think its designers planned on it becoming the landmark tourist attraction that it is today?

On the other hand, remember there are still Roman roads and aqueducts in use today, thousands of years after their construction. Roman engineers knew what they were doing. They were among the people who recognize the need to assemble their tools, prepare the ground, and lay foundations ahead of time. They'll do the "little work" early, so that the "big work" is easier to do later. Once that's done, nature or other tradespeople can do the rest of the work in confidence.

Do we listen to words or watch actions and results? Are you one of those people who under-promises and over-delivers – or who just makes empty promises because you think it's what your audience wants to hear? Never forget to keep that big picture in mind. It's there to guide your brush strokes [or pixel placement].

Verse 64

Prevent problems before they can rise.

Verse 64 is simply an extension of the verse 63. It also contains the famous "journey of 1,000 miles" line that so many of us pay lip service to. Most of us understand it in terms of taking that first step on a big project: recognizing that we can't have a meal unless someone's planted a seed, harvested the plant and cooked the food. Another way to look at it is to be aware of our surroundings and their potential. That journey of 1,000 miles might also be the best one to undertake if the emperor's troops are on their way to collect you. [You may be familiar with a bible story about King Herod's men searching for a family with a newborn infant...]

While it's good to save, it's better to invest. If you store all your seeds for some time in the future, all you'll really do is feed some mice. You'll find another version of this in *Matthew 25:14-30*.

Use judgement, create balance, look to the future. If you nurture a project while it's young and defenseless, it will grow to where it doesn't need you – and maybe even pay you back.

If you don't know where you're going, how will you know you've arrived?

Verse 66

To lead people, walk behind them.

The mark of any successful politician, salesman or teacher is convincing people that they share a common experience and goal – that they've been in their audience's shoes. If people see their own potential in your success, you'll have a lot more credibility. To recall comedian George Burns: "Sincerity is everything – if you can fake that, you've got it made."

Ideally you can achieve this through true humility, where people can see who you are and how you got there without your having to wave it in their face. If they can accept you in this manner, you've succeeded. If they see what appears to be your "success" as something they'd like as opposed to something they already have through you, you're creating desire and possible jealousy.

The solution? Remember you've got two ears, two eyes and one mouth. Try to use them in that proportion. Be humble and respectful, giving people reasons and examples on how to emulate you without replacing you. If you're part of their tribe or family, their strength is yours and your strength is theirs.

Verse 71

Knowing you don't know makes you whole.
Thinking you know everything is a disease.

At this point most of us are looking at knowledge that comes from our human experience. To appreciate it from the Taoist experience, we'll want to place ourselves in the environment that exists outside of our brains and bodies: the world and universe we inhabit. What works well indoors is many times useless outdoors. A scientist can tell you of all the similarities involved in moving through water and air. Common sense tells us to respect the differences. Water and air may be the same to the academic full of their own cleverness, but they're different to people living in the real world, outside the classroom's confines.

In other words, don't let your ego – your supreme confidence in everything you do and have – get in the way of learning – and respecting who and what you don't know.

Verse 72

When people have no more fear...

There once was a time when the term fear meant respect. Like many words in many languages, it can convey more than one meaning. In contemporary English it has become more identified with dread and terror. In biblical translations drawn from the Greek, the word *phobos* [which carries both meanings, with translation depending on context] came to us as today's fear. Whether you want to respect or be afraid of your creator is a theological discussion we'll leave for another time and place.

In *Tao*'s context, where we want to live in harmony with our natural environment – which includes other people – terms like fear and awe are divisive. To get things done, it's preferable to be a person people emulate and respect rather than one who fills them with terror. We all have strengths and weaknesses. If others have a talent for doing what we cannot, wonderful. Our job is simply to provide an environment for them to do what they do best – and hopefully they'll learn enough from our behavior to do their best for society and not for greed.

Your power doesn't lie in strength, but in not needing to use your strength.

Verse 81

True words may not sound beautiful. Beautiful sounding words may not be true.

In today's society we find that many of the *Tao*'s verses need interpretation, rather than translation. Hopefully my responses to *Tao*'s truths have helped you on your journey. If you've agreed with me, wonderful. If your disagreement has led you to new insights about yourself, wonderful. We all have our own path – our own *Tao* – and you'll want to be sure you're on your own course, not mine or anyone else's.

Now it's time to find your own translation of the *Tao Te Ching*. Read the last verse. Think of examples you've encountered in your life.

OK. What's your path looking like now?

ACKNOWLEDGEMENTS

This book wouldn't exist without the help of everyone I've encountered along my personal *Tao*.

If we've ever met in person, you've contributed to this book. Even if we've never met in person, if you've ever said, written or somehow done something that's influenced me, you've contributed to this book. If you've ever done something that influenced those people, places and conditions that have influenced me, much like the proverbial butterfly who affects lives half a world away, you've contributed to this book.

More recently I owe sincere thanks to Fr. Giuseppe, OFM, a Brazilian cleric who's helped me in more ways than I can possibly name. To LaVon Blaesi, whose beautiful gift book started this part of my journey. Barbara Brodsky, Robert Jacobs, Terri McClernon, Tavis Taylor and other members of the Deep Spring Sangha who've encouraged me as this book evolved into its present form over the years. And even though I've spent a lifetime perfecting the art of procrastination, there are people like Mel Murphy and Norah Desmond who've kept me on track. I still recall bumping into Norah on a city street after not seeing each other for nearly a year. And the first words that accompanied her big smile? "How's the book coming along?" My embarrassed answer at the time was that I hadn't touched it, much less thought about it, since we'd last talked.

As the final edits came together, Mícheál Garvey, Carmel Moore and Linda Nicholson shared their years of experience, study and travel with invaluable comments. You gave me the objective outside perspective that's essential to any project that evolves as this one did. Paul Murray offered the common-sense advice I needed in setting up the website. Agnieszka "Aggie" Jankowska and Michael Cusack polished my preconceived, but not-quite-right, thoughts to produce this printed book in the form that finally saw the light of day and the eyes of readers.

To every one of you, thank you. Here's the result of your help, your questions, your encouragement. Please take credit for all you like and let me take responsibility for anything that's not to your taste.

Source Verses

The quotes at the beginning of each section in this book come from a synthesis of my years of research. My goal has been to use contemporary English to reflect the sense of the particular verse – or portion of a verse – that's an essay's subject. There are many outstanding editions of the *Tao Te Ching*. If a particular section grabs your attention in any way, please find an edition of the *Tao* that resonates with you. While these are the verses that spoke most clearly to me, you may have a totally different take on them.

For those of you who'd like to form your own judgements to create your own path – your own version of this book – here are my sources:

Verses by topic

The Sage draws on 26 of the *Tao's* 81 verses. I've used verses 2, 3, 5, 7, 12, 22, 26, 27, 29, 47, 49, 57, 58, 60, 63, 64, 66, 68, 70, 71, 72, 73, 77, 78, 79, and 81.

Te, or Virtue, is sourced in 13 verses: 10, 21, 28, 38, 41, 49, 51, 54, 55, 59, 60, 68, and 79.

Wu-Wei, or non-action, uses these 21 verses: 2, 3, 8, 11, 15, 30, 34, 37, 38, 41, 43, 47, 48, 57, 58, 63, 64, 66, 71, 72, and 81.

Topics by Verse

Book 1
Book of the Way

2 – Sage, Wu-Wei
3 – Sage, Wu-Wei
5 – Sage
7 – Sage
8 – Wu-Wei
10 – Te
11 – Wu-Wei
12 – Sage
15 – Wu-Wei
21 – Te
22 – Sage
26 – Sage
27 – Sage
28 – Te
29 – Sage
30 – Wu-Wei
34 – Wu-Wei
37 – Wu-Wei

Book 2
Book of Virtue

38 – Te, Wu-Wei
41 – Te, Wu-Wei
43 – Wu-Wei
47 – Sage, Wu-Wei
48 – Wu-Wei
49 – Sage, Te
51 – Te
54 – Te
55 – Te
57 – Sage, Wu-Wei
58 – Sage, Wu-Wei
59 – Te
60 – Sage, Te
63 – Sage, Wu-Wei
64 – Sage, Wu-Wei
66 – Sage, Wu-Wei
68 – Sage, Te
70 – Sage
71 – Sage, Wu-Wei
72 – Sage, Wu-Wei
73 – Sage
77 – Sage
78 – Sage
79 – Sage, Te
81 – Sage, Wu-Wei

Social Media Notes

There's more to the *Tao Te Ching* than you've seen in this book. Lots more. And there's also lots more to this book's approach than you've seen in these pages.

On our website you'll find occasional updates to the book's content, as well as a *Galleries* section, with aphorisms tied to each of the *Tao's* 81 verses. You'll also find sections that show how the *Tao* appears in the Bible, Shakespeare and the works of a number of people you might not instantly identify as Taoist.
https://yourdayyourtao.org/

We also post regularly on Twitter and Facebook, where you can follow us to see images from our website in your feed.

https://twitter.com/YourDayYourTao

https://twitter.com/ShakespearesTao

https://www.facebook.com/Your-Day-Your-Tao/

https://www.facebook.com/ShakespearesTao/

About the author

James Patrick Maney, also known as Jim or JP, depending on the many different circles he's traveling in, has been fortunate enough to combine several careers into a single lifetime.

His life journey has taken him around the world, from factory floors and wilderness backpacking to an advertising and public relations career that brought him into corporate boardrooms and university teaching. Along the way he's learned from indigenous elders, spiritual teachers and businessmen large and small. He draws on these experiences and uses the *Tao Te Ching* as a tool to help us integrate the many roles we all play in life. Maney ties the *Tao's* messages together in a way that makes them accessible and useful. You can learn more about his travels at https://jpmaney.com/ and his approach to the *Tao Te Ching* at https://yourdayyourtao.org/

So you made your day your Tao

Have a great day

an cosán press
info@yourdayyourtao.org

www.ingramcontent.com/pod-product-compliance
Lightning Source LLC
Chambersburg PA
CBHW070900080526
44589CB00013B/1150